TAAS MASTER

Student Practice Book
Reading Grade 3

Practice Material
for the
Texas Assessment of Academic Skills
Reading Objectives

ECS
Learning Systems
INC.

Dear Educator:

ECS Learning Systems, Inc., a Texas company based in San Antonio, is the leading publisher of TAAS practice materials. Since 1982, ECS has been providing superior teacher materials and workshops. We will continue our commitment to bring you innovative ideas to challenge, motivate, and instruct your students.

We appreciate the wonderful comments we receive from our valued customers. We look forward to hearing from you.

Best wishes,

Your friends at ECS

TAAS MASTER™ Practice Test Class Packs
A great diagnostic and practice tool
Available in mathematics, reading, and writing for all tested grades

- Use TAAS MASTER™ Practice Tests to diagnose students' strengths and weaknesses.
- Use TAAS MASTER™ books with students who need more practice.
- TAAS MASTER™ Practice Tests and TAAS MASTER™ books help teachers build a complete TAAS preparation program for students when used as part of a strong instructional program.

ECS Learning Systems, Inc.
P.O. Box 791437
San Antonio, Texas 78279-1437

Editor: Lori Mammen
Page Layout & Graphics: Barbara Biel
Cover/Book Design: Educational Media Services

ISBN 1-57022-080-8

Table of Contents

Introduction   5

How to Use This Book   5

Instructional Targets   7

Domain: Reading Comprehension   9

Practice Passages   11

   Birbal and the Six Foolish People (Part 1)   11

   Birbal and the Six Foolish People (Part 2)   15

   Forests of the World   19

   Who was Leonardo da Vinci?   23

   An Old, Old Game   27

   Who was Sojourner Truth?   31

   Food Named After People   35

   Why Crabs Dig in the Sand   39

   A New Way to Study   43

   Fly Away Home   47

   What kind of pet is it?   51

   First-Class Snack   55

   How much do you know about the bluebonnet?   59

   Flying a Kite—The Safe Way   63

   An Unusual Fish   67

   The City Mouse and the Country Mouse   71

   The Butterfly World   75

   The Boy Who Cried "Wolf"   79

Answer Key   83

Credits

Page 55, "First-Class Snack," by Anne Leinster and Family, from COBBLESTONE's May, 1985 issue: *The U.S. Postal Service*, © 1985, Cobblestone Publishing, Inc., 7 School St., Peterborough, NH 03458. Reprinted by permission of the publisher.

Introduction

This book is designed to provide appropriate practice material for the reading portion of the Texas Assessment of Academic Skills (TAAS). The material in this book relates directly to the content of the TAAS, and the exercises have been designed to meet the requirements of the test. In addition, the exercises reflect the interests and experiences of third-grade students. Your students will find the material in this book both interesting and motivating.

The book contains review exercises that focus on the objectives and instructional targets of the TAAS. These exercises provide opportunities to assess students' understanding and mastery of the various test objectives. Students also gain experience in the format of the questions that might appear on the TAAS.

How to Use This Book

This book provides exercises for a quick review of the objectives found on TAAS. Third-grade teachers and students may use the exercises during the regular school year or during tutorial sessions.

The book contains several reading passages followed by questions. The questions are identified by the instructional target and objective which they address. In addition, each reading passage is preceded by a summary page that provides a brief overview for the teacher. It lists the following information: the passage's title, number of words in the passage, and instructional targets addressed in the passage. This information allows the teacher to select passages most appropriate for his/her students' needs.

Teachers will find that each objective/instructional target is addressed several times throughout the book. This lets students practice in a variety of contexts.

Several readability formulas were used to determine the readability of each passage. All passages are appropriate for third-grade readers.

Objectives and Instructional Targets—Grade 3 Reading

Domain: Reading Comprehension

Objective 1: The student will determine the meaning of words in a variety of written texts.

- Use knowledge of the meanings of prefixes and suffixes to determine word meanings
- Use context clues to determine the meanings of unfamiliar words
- Use context clues to determine the meanings of specialized/technical terms

Objective 2: The student will identify supporting ideas in a variety of written texts.

- Recall supporting facts and details
- Arrange events in sequential order
- Follow written directions
- Describe the setting of a story (time and place)

Objective 3: The student will summarize a variety of written texts.

- Identify the stated or paraphrased main idea of a selection
- Identify the best summary of a selection

Objective 4: The student will perceive relationships and recognize outcomes in a variety of written texts.

- Identify cause and effect relationships
- Predict probable future actions and outcomes

Objective 5: The student will analyze information in a variety of written texts in order to make inferences and generalizations.

- Understand the feelings and emotions of characters

Objective 6: The student will recognize points of view, propaganda, and/or statements of fact and nonfact in a variety of written texts.

- Distinguish between fact and nonfact

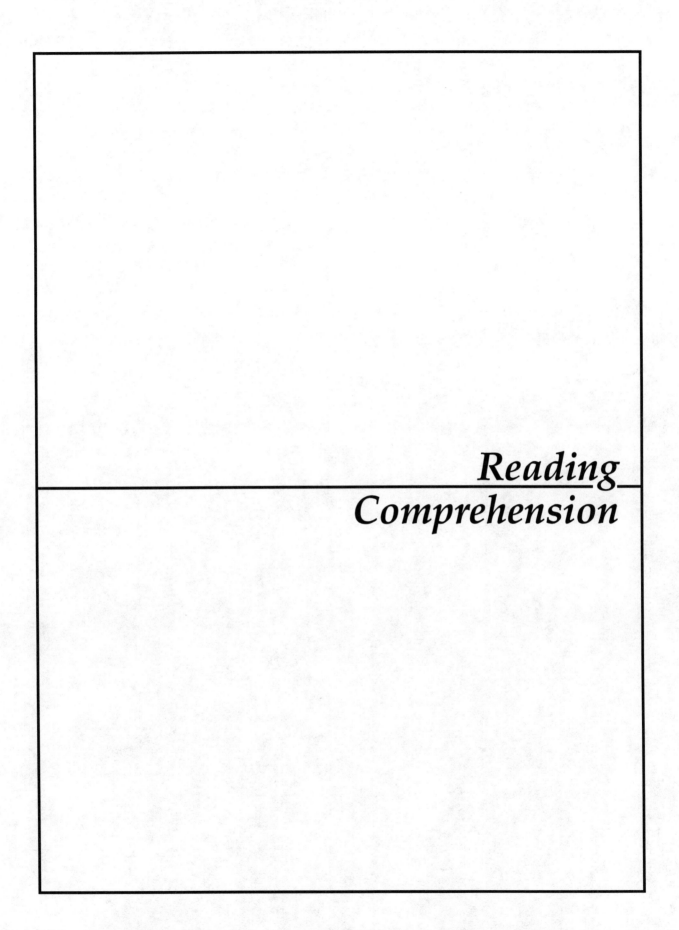

Reading Comprehension

Title: Birbal and the Six Foolish People (Part 1)

Number of Words: 500

Objectives/Instructional Targets:

Objective 1:

- ☑ Use knowledge of the meanings of prefixes and suffixes to determine word meanings
- ☑ Use context clues to determine the meanings of unfamiliar words
- ☐ Use context clues to determine the meanings of specialized/technical terms

Objective 2:

- ☑ Recall supporting facts and details
- ☑ Arrange events in sequential order
- ☐ Follow written directions
- ☑ Describe the setting of a story (time and place)

Objective 3:

- ☐ Identify the stated or paraphrased main idea of a selection
- ☑ Identify the best summary of a selection

Objective 4:

- ☑ Identify cause and effect relationships
- ☑ Predict probable future outcomes

Objective 5:

- ☑ Understand the feelings and emotions of characters

Objective 6:

- ☐ Distinguish between fact and nonfact

Birbal and the Six Foolish People (Part 1)

The folklore of India includes many stories about two popular characters, Akbar, a great king of India, and his faithful servant, Birbal. This passage retells one of their stories.

Once upon a time in India, there was a king named Akbar. He was a strong and fair king, but sometimes he had strange ideas. Then he would ask members of his court to do difficult things. One day, Akbar said, "Every day I see smart people all around me. For a change, I want to see some foolish people."

His faithful servant Birbal said, "I will find six foolish people."

"Fine," said Akbar, "you have one month to bring me six fools."

"Oh, I don't need one month," answered Birbal.

The next day, Birbal set out to find six foolish people. He hadn't gone far in the city when he saw a man standing up to his knees in a mud puddle. The man's arms were stretched stiffly out to his sides. He tried to get out of the mud, but he could not.

"Do you need help, sir?" Birbal asked the man.

"Oh, yes," the man answered.

"Give me your hand. I will pull you from the mud," said Birbal.

"I can't give you my hand. My wife wants a pot this big. If I give you my hand, I will not know what size pot to buy," said the man. "Just pull me out by my hair."

Birbal grabbed the man's hair and pulled him from the mud. Then he wrote the man's name and address on a paper and put it in his pocket. "Here is my first foolish person," Birbal said to himself. Then he continued on his search.

Before long, Birbal met a man riding a horse. The man also carried a bale of hay on his head.

"Excuse me," Birbal said to the man. "Why do you have that bale of hay on your head?"

"Oh, my horse is very old and tired. I am sure that this bale of hay is much too heavy for him to carry, so I carry it on my head," the man answered.

Birbal just shook his head as he added the man's name and address to his paper. He had found his second foolish person.

Birbal continued walking and turned down a very narrow street. Suddenly, a man <u>dashed</u> toward him. The man crashed into Birbal and knocked him down on the <u>pavement</u>.

"What is the matter with you?" screamed Birbal. "Didn't you see me walking here?"

"Oh, I am so sorry, sir, but you got in my way. If you had moved aside, I could have caught it," answered the man.

Birbal looked around, but saw nothing. "What were you trying to catch?" he asked the man.

"I had just said my evening prayers from that church over there. I was running to see how far my voice could reach. You ruined my chance, because you were in my way," the man explained.

"This is just too easy," Birbal laughed to himself. "Imagine a man chasing his own voice down the street!" He added the man's name and address to his paper and continued down the street.

Unfamiliar Words (1)

1. In this passage, the word <u>dashed</u> means—

   ○ walked slowly
   ○ stood still
   ○ jumped high
   ○ ran quickly

Prefixes/Suffixes (1)

2. What does the word <u>pavement</u> mean in this story?

   ○ Church steps
   ○ Street
   ○ Mud
   ○ Floor

Facts/Details (2)

3. The first foolish man that Birbal met was—

   ○ working in the king's court
   ○ riding a horse
   ○ standing in a mud puddle
   ○ buying a pot at the market

Sequential Order (2)

4. Which event happened first in the story?

   ○ Birbal met a man riding a horse.
   ○ Akbar said he wanted to see some foolish people.
   ○ Birbal wrote the man's name on a paper.
   ○ Birbal pulled the man from a mud puddle.

Setting of Story (2)

5. Where did most of this part of the story happen?

   - ○ On the streets of an Indian city
   - ○ On a farm
   - ○ At Akbar's castle
   - ○ At Birbal's house

Best Summary (3)

6. Which is the best summary of this part of the story?

   - ○ Akbar becomes a strong and fair king in India.
   - ○ A man stands in a mud puddle and cannot get out.
   - ○ Birbal meets a foolish man who carries a bale of hay on his head.
   - ○ Akbar's servant, Birbal, sets out to find six foolish people for the king.

Cause/Effect (4)

7. The man on the narrow street knocked Birbal down because he—

   - ○ wanted to prove he was not foolish
   - ○ did not like Birbal
   - ○ was trying to catch his voice
   - ○ was late getting to his church

Predicting Outcomes (4)

8. Which of the following is Birbal most likely to do next?

   - ○ Tell Akbar he could not find any foolish people
   - ○ Continue looking for more foolish people
   - ○ Tell the three men that they are foolish
   - ○ Chase the foolish man who knocked him down

Feelings/Emotions of Characters (5)

9. Birbal seems to think that finding six foolish people will be—

   - ○ difficult
   - ○ dangerous
   - ○ scary
   - ○ easy

Feelings/Emotions of Characters (5)

10. How did the man feel after he knocked Birbal down?

    - ○ Sorry
    - ○ Embarrassed
    - ○ Disappointed
    - ○ Foolish

Title: Birbal and the Six Foolish People (Part 2)

Number of Words: 457

Objectives/Instructional Targets:

Objective 1:

- ☑ Use knowledge of the meanings of prefixes and suffixes to determine word meanings
- ☑ Use context clues to determine the meanings of unfamiliar words
- ☐ Use context clues to determine the meanings of specialized/technical terms

Objective 2:

- ☐ Recall supporting facts and details
- ☑ Arrange events in sequential order
- ☐ Follow written directions
- ☑ Describe the setting of a story (time and place)

Objective 3:

- ☐ Identify the stated or paraphrased main idea of a selection
- ☐ Identify the best summary of a selection

Objective 4:

- ☑ Identify cause and effect relationships
- ☐ Predict probable future outcomes

Objective 5:

- ☑ Understand the feelings and emotions of characters

Objective 6:

- ☐ Distinguish between fact and nonfact

Birbal and the Six Foolish People (Part 2)

Birbal had been out for several hours. It was now dark, and the street lights were burning brightly. In the distance, Birbal saw a man crawling on the ground under one of the street lights. He was obviously looking for something.

"Sir, did you lose something?" Birbal asked as he <u>approached</u> the man.

"Oh, my, yes! I have lost my diamond ring!" cried the man.

"Did you lose it right here?" asked Birbal.

"Oh, no. I lost it over there," the man said as he pointed to a park across the street. "But it is dark over there. It is easier to look for it in the bright light."

Birbal could not believe how foolish this man was. He lost his ring in a park, but he looked for it under a street light. Birbal could not believe his good <u>fortune</u> to find a fourth foolish person. He added the man's name and address to his list. Now it was very dark, indeed. Birbal decided to go home and rest. He would take his list to Akbar in the morning.

The next morning Birbal rose early and went straight to Akbar's court.

"Have you found six foolish people, Birbal?" asked Akbar.

"Yes, your majesty!" said Birbal. "And it was much easier than I thought it would be." Then Birbal gave his list of foolish people to a messenger and told him to bring them to Akbar's court.

One by one, the foolish people arrived at Akbar's court. As each one arrived, Birbal introduced him and told the story of his foolish acts. After each story, Akbar nodded his head in satisfaction. Indeed, Birbal had found some very foolish people!

When Birbal had finished the introductions and stories, Akbar looked around. Something was not right.

"Birbal, you promised to bring me six foolish people. I can easily count that there are only four. You have not <u>fulfilled</u> your promise," Akbar said.

"Pardon me, your majesty, but I have <u>fulfilled</u> my promise. I have brought four foolish people to your court, but there are two more," Birbal smiled at Akbar.

"Then, where are they, Birbal?" demanded the king.

"We are the other two foolish people, your majesty. You are a foolish person for <u>conceiving</u> of such an idea. And I am a foolish person for obeying you!" Birbal laughed.

Akbar looked angrily at Birbal, but the other members of the court began to laugh at Birbal's joke. They laughed and laughed, until the entire room was filled with their uproar. Akbar could not help himself, and he, too, began to laugh. Birbal had pulled off a very funny prank!

The four other foolish people received gifts from Akbar, and Birbal was the star of the king's court for many days.

Prefixes/Suffixes (1)

1. In this passage, the word <u>approached</u> means—

   ○ went away
   ○ stood still
   ○ went near
   ○ hid from

Unfamiliar Words (1)

2. What does the word <u>fortune</u> mean in this passage?

   ○ Behavior
   ○ Writing
   ○ Luck
   ○ Thinking

Prefixes/Suffixes (1)

3. In this passage, what does the word <u>fulfilled</u> mean?

   ○ Kept
   ○ Forgotten
   ○ Found
   ○ Spoken

Unfamiliar Words (1)

4. In this passage, the word <u>conceiving</u> means—

   ○ remembering
   ○ looking for
   ○ missing
   ○ thinking of

Unfamiliar Words (1)

5. In this passage, the word <u>prank</u> means—

   ○ answer
   ○ trick
   ○ laugh
   ○ list

Sequential Order (2)

6. Which of the following happened right after Birbal introduced the four foolish men?

   ○ Akbar began to laugh at the foolish men.
   ○ Birbal became the star of the king's court.
   ○ Akbar looked around for the two missing foolish people.
   ○ Birbal sent the messenger to find the last two foolish men.

Setting of Story (2)

7. When did Akbar meet the foolish men that Birbal found?

   ○ Late at night
   ○ Many days after Birbal found them
   ○ The same day Birbal found them
   ○ The day after Birbal found them

Cause/Effect (4)

8. The members of Akbar's court laughed because they—

   ○ knew Akbar was angry at Birbal
   ○ thought Birbal's prank was funny
   ○ had never met foolish people
   ○ wanted to fill the room with laughter

Feelings/Emotions of Characters (5)

9. Other members of Akbar's court probably thought that Birbal's prank was—

   ○ clever
   ○ foolish
   ○ stupid
   ○ dangerous

Feelings/Emotions of Characters (5)

10. How did Birbal feel after he found the fourth foolish person?

    ○ Foolish
    ○ Frightened
    ○ Lucky
    ○ Proud

Title: Forests of the World

Number of Words: 314

Objectives/Instructional Targets:

Objective 1:

- ☑ Use knowledge of the meanings of prefixes and suffixes to determine word meanings
- ☑ Use context clues to determine the meanings of unfamiliar words
- ☑ Use context clues to determine the meanings of specialized/technical terms

Objective 2:

- ☑ Recall supporting facts and details
- ☐ Arrange events in sequential order
- ☐ Follow written directions
- ☐ Describe the setting of a story (time and place)

Objective 3:

- ☑ Identify the stated or paraphrased main idea of a selection
- ☐ Identify the best summary of a selection

Objective 4:

- ☑ Identify cause and effect relationships
- ☑ Predict probable future outcomes

Objective 5:

- ☐ Understand the feelings and emotions of characters

Objective 6:

- ☑ Distinguish between fact and nonfact

Forests of the World

What is a forest? You may think of the forest in a fairy tale. Fairy tale forests are usually dark, scary places. There are other kinds of forests in the world. In fact, forests cover about one-fourth of the earth's land.

Evergreen forests grow in the northern parts of the world. Evergreen forests have trees that are always green. The evergreen trees are called conifers. Conifers never shed their leaves, which are called needles. A waxy coating covers the needles. This protects them from cold weather. A conifer also makes cones. The cones hold the tree's seeds. As the cones grow, they open and drop their seeds to the ground. Two common conifers are fir and spruce trees.

Deciduous forests grow south of the evergreen forests. These forests have trees like poplars, maples, and oaks. These trees lose their leaves during the winter. The leaves cannot survive in very cold places because there is not enough sunlight. The leaves change color and drop from the trees when there is less sunlight in the fall. The trees live without their leaves until spring. Then they make new leaves.

Rain forests grow in hot, wet areas in places like South America and India. The trees in a rain forest are always green. They grow tall and close together. They make a "blanket of green" that towers above the ground. Rain forests are the most important forests on the earth. They play an important part in making oxygen for the earth. A rain forest may have thousands of different trees. One common type is the rubber tree.

All forests help us. The forests' trees give material for many things we use each day. Trees also keep the earth cool. Like other green plants, trees give us oxygen to breathe. Oxygen is a gas that people need to breathe. Without forests, people would find life much harder.

Specialized/Technical Terms (1)

1. In this passage, the word <u>conifers</u> means trees that—

   ○ grow in forests
   ○ lose their leaves
   ○ have seeds
   ○ make cones

Specialized/Technical Terms (1)

2. In this passage, the word <u>deciduous</u> describes trees that—

   ○ have needles
   ○ lose their leaves in winter
   ○ grow in rain forests
   ○ give us oxygen

Unfamiliar Words (1)

3. What does the word <u>towers</u> mean in this passage?

   ○ Stands tall
   ○ Cools
   ○ Gives
   ○ Stays green

Prefixes/Suffixes (1)

4. What does the word <u>coating</u> mean in this passage?

   ○ leaf
   ○ layer
   ○ cone
   ○ needle

Facts/Details (2)

5. Which of the following trees grows in a rain forest?

   ○ Spruce tree
   ○ Oak tree
   ○ Rubber tree
   ○ Poplar tree

Facts/Details (2)

6. The leaves on conifers are called—

   ○ cones
   ○ seeds
   ○ needles
   ○ firs

Stated/Paraphrased Main Idea (3)

7. This passage is mostly about—

    ○ why people need oxygen
    ○ why forests are dark and scary
    ○ how trees live through the winter
    ○ the different kinds of forests in the world

Cause/Effect (4)

8. The needles on an evergreen tree are protected from the cold because the needles—

    ○ grow near the cones
    ○ drop seeds on the ground
    ○ are always green
    ○ have a waxy coating

Predicting Outcomes (4)

9. What would probably happen if there were no trees?

    ○ There would be no oxygen on the earth.
    ○ People would have to find new material to make some of the things they use.
    ○ There would be no green plants left on the earth.
    ○ The earth would become very cold.

Fact/Nonfact (6)

10. Which is an OPINION in the passage?

    ○ Rain forests are the most important forests on the earth.
    ○ Forests cover about one-fourth of the earth's land.
    ○ Oxygen is a gas that people need to breathe.
    ○ A rain forest may have thousands of different trees.

Title: Who was Leonardo da Vinci?

Number of Words: 367

Objectives/Instructional Targets:

Objective 1:

- ☑ Use knowledge of the meanings of prefixes and suffixes to determine word meanings
- ☑ Use context clues to determine the meanings of unfamiliar words
- ☐ Use context clues to determine the meanings of specialized/technical terms

Objective 2:

- ☑ Recall supporting facts and details
- ☐ Arrange events in sequential order
- ☐ Follow written directions
- ☐ Describe the setting of a story (time and place)

Objective 3:

- ☑ Identify the stated or paraphrased main idea of a selection
- ☐ Identify the best summary of a selection

Objective 4:

- ☑ Identify cause and effect relationships
- ☐ Predict probable future outcomes

Objective 5:

- ☐ Understand the feelings and emotions of characters

Objective 6:

- ☑ Distinguish between fact and nonfact

Who was Leonardo da Vinci?

He was a famous artist and painter. He was probably one of the greatest painters in history. He was also an <u>inventor.</u> He designed hundreds of machines and <u>gadgets.</u> Most of his inventions were only drawings on paper. He never made most of his ideas, but some of them gave us the plans for our modern machines.

Da Vinci was born in Florence, Italy, in 1452. As a young man, he was a talented painter. People around the world know about his most famous painting. It is called the *Mona Lisa.* Painting was only one of the things that da Vinci liked to do. He knew about much, much more. He knew about buildings, geography, the stars, and the planets, to name only a few. He always looked for easier and better ways to do things, too.

For some of his ideas, da Vinci looked far into the future. He <u>foresaw</u> a time and a world that others could not even imagine. He drew a machine that many people think was the first helicopter. His "armored car" was hundreds of years ahead of its time. Like a modern tank, it could carry cannons inside of it. Da Vinci did not limit himself to land travel. One of his most interesting inventions was a paddle-wheel boat. It did not need oars to move it through the water.

Da Vinci's drawings and plans included many different machines. His spinning wheel let a worker spin and wind the thread at the same time. Another machine let a diver stay underwater for long periods of time. The diver breathed through a tube. The tube brought air from above the water to the diver below.

Do you like to go to the movies? Over 500 years ago, da Vinci drew a plan for a movie projector. It used a candle for light and <u>cast</u> a large picture on the wall. We use the same idea to show movies today.

Da Vinci had many, many wonderful ideas—from transportation to home improvement to entertainment. They included a mechanical car and a parachute. All of them show just how creative Leonardo da Vinci was.

Leonardo da Vinci

Prefixes/Suffixes (1)

1. What does the word <u>inventor</u> mean in this passage?

   ⬭ A person who is famous
   ⬭ A person who creates new machines
   ⬭ A person who paints
   ⬭ A person who travels

Unfamiliar Words (1)

2. In this passage, the word <u>gadgets</u> means—

   ⬭ paintings
   ⬭ drawings
   ⬭ machines
   ⬭ ideas

Prefixes/Suffixes (1)

3. In this passage, the word <u>foresaw</u> means—

   ⬭ saw later
   ⬭ saw beforehand
   ⬭ did not see
   ⬭ looked back to

Unfamiliar Words (1)

4. What does the word <u>cast</u> mean in this passage?

   ⬭ Hid
   ⬭ Drew
   ⬭ Burned
   ⬭ Created

Facts/Details (2)

5. In addition to being an inventor, Leonardo da Vinci was also a—

   ⬭ farmer
   ⬭ soldier
   ⬭ painter
   ⬭ diver

Stated/Paraphrased Main Idea (3)

6. This passage is mostly about—

   ⬭ how da Vinci became a great artist
   ⬭ why da Vinci's inventions did not succeed
   ⬭ how da Vinci's inventions have changed in 500 years
   ⬭ some of da Vinci's creative inventions

Cause/Effect (4)

7. According to the passage, da Vinci invented things because he—

   ○ did not enjoy painting
   ○ wanted easier and better ways to do things
   ○ knew no one else had good ideas
   ○ could never make most of his ideas

Fact/Nonfact (6)

8. Which is an OPINION in this passage?

   ○ Leonardo da Vinci had many, many wonderful ideas.
   ○ Leonardo da Vinci was a painter and an inventor.
   ○ Leonardo da Vinci lived more than 500 years ago.
   ○ Leonardo da Vinci made each of his inventions.

Fact/Nonfact (6)

9. Which is a FACT in this passage?

   ○ Leonardo da Vinci was one of the greatest painters in history.
   ○ Leonardo da Vinci knew the easiest and best way to work.
   ○ Leonardo da Vinci was born in Florence, Italy.
   ○ Leonardo da Vinci's most wonderful invention was the movie projector.

Title: An Old, Old Game

Number of Words: 482

Objectives/Instructional Targets:

Objective 1:

- ☐ Use knowledge of the meanings of prefixes and suffixes to determine word meanings
- ☑ Use context clues to determine the meanings of unfamiliar words
- ☑ Use context clues to determine the meanings of specialized/technical terms

Objective 2:

- ☑ Recall supporting facts and details
- ☐ Arrange events in sequential order
- ☐ Follow written directions
- ☐ Describe the setting of a story (time and place)

Objective 3:

- ☑ Identify the stated or paraphrased main idea of a selection
- ☐ Identify the best summary of a selection

Objective 4:

- ☑ Identify cause and effect relationships
- ☐ Predict probable future outcomes

Objective 5:

- ☐ Understand the feelings and emotions of characters

Objective 6:

- ☑ Distinguish between fact and nonfact

An Old, Old Game

What is chess?

Chess is a game for two players. They play the game on a square chessboard. The board looks like a checkerboard. At the start of the game, each player has 16 pieces to control and move. There are six different kinds of pieces. Each kind has a special name: king, queen, pawn, bishop, knight, and <u>rook</u> (castle).

The game is like a war between the two players' pieces. When countries are at war, the leaders want to <u>defeat</u> their enemy. In chess, players want to defeat their enemy, too. They move their pieces like an invasion. The "war" is won when one player captures the other player's king. This is called "checkmate."

Why is chess a thinking game?

The rules for chess are easy, but a player can always improve. There are many ways to win the game. As players improve, they learn new ways to win the game. There are books about chess. These books explain some of the <u>strategies</u> for winning the game. Learning the <u>strategies</u> can take a long time. To play the game well, though, a player must think hard and know a lot about the game.

How has chess changed?

People have played chess for hundreds of years. It began in the Indus Valley of India. As time passed, the game spread around the world. Travelers learned the game and then took it back to their homes.

A chess set is the chessboard and all the pieces. The board and pieces can be like works of art. Many chess sets are very fancy. People have made chess sets from many different materials. There are boards and pieces made from wood or ivory. Others are made from bone, gold, silver, or crystal. Today most chess sets are wooden or plastic. There are also electronic chess sets. Some of these sets let one person play the game alone.

Who plays chess?

At first only royalty (kings and princes) and rich people played chess. Finally, other people could play the game, too. As the game spread, it changed and improved. People began to have chess contests. The contests were called <u>tournaments.</u> They held <u>tournaments</u> to find out who were the best players.

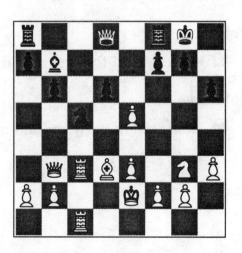

The first big chess <u>tournament</u> was in London, England. Adolf Anderssen, a German man, won this first contest. After a major <u>tournament</u> in Russia, the winner earned the title of "grandmaster." Today, anyone who wins a chess <u>tournament</u> is still called a grandmaster.

Paul Morphy was the first American chess champion. He was a great player. Morphy beat most of the great players from Europe. In fact, he never lost a game. Bobby Fischer was another famous chess champion. He learned to play chess when he was six years old. He was only 13 years old when he became the junior chess champion of the United States. He was the youngest grandmaster of all time.

Unfamiliar Words (1)

1. In this passage, the word <u>defeat</u> means—

   ○ like
   ○ help
   ○ beat
   ○ win

Specialized/Technical Terms (1)

2. What does the word <u>rook</u> mean in this passage?

   ○ King
   ○ Castle
   ○ Pawn
   ○ Piece

Unfamiliar Words (1)

3. In this passage, the word <u>strategies</u> means—

   ○ chess books
   ○ chess sets
   ○ players
   ○ careful plans

Specialized/Technical Terms (1)

4. In this passage, the word <u>tournaments</u> means—

   ○ best players
   ○ chess contests
   ○ kings and princes
   ○ people who play chess

Facts/Details (2)

5. What is it called when a player captures another player's king?

- ◯ Grandmaster
- ◯ Strategies
- ◯ Capture
- ◯ Checkmate

Facts/Details (2)

6. Where did the game of chess begin?

- ◯ England
- ◯ Germany
- ◯ India
- ◯ United States

Stated/Paraphrased Main Idea (3)

7. The second paragraph is mostly about—

- ◯ how to win a chess game
- ◯ how to capture a player's queen
- ◯ why chess is like a war
- ◯ why two people must play chess

Cause/Effect (4)

8. The game of chess spread around the world because—

- ◯ Bobby Fischer taught people how to play
- ◯ travelers took the game back to their homes
- ◯ it began in the Indus Valley
- ◯ it changed as time passed

Fact/Nonfact (6)

9. Which is a FACT in this passage?

- ◯ The rules for chess are easy.
- ◯ Chess is played like checkers.
- ◯ Only royalty can play chess.
- ◯ Paul Morphy was the first American chess champion.

Fact/Nonfact (6)

10. Which is an OPINION in this passage?

- ◯ Chess is a game for two players.
- ◯ Paul Morphy was a great player.
- ◯ Bobby Fischer was the youngest grandmaster.
- ◯ There are six different kinds of chess pieces.

Title: Who was Sojourner Truth?

Number of Words: 484

Objectives/Instructional Targets:

Objective 1:

- ☑ Use knowledge of the meanings of prefixes and suffixes to determine word meanings
- ☑ Use context clues to determine the meanings of unfamiliar words
- ☐ Use context clues to determine the meanings of specialized/technical terms

Objective 2:

- ☑ Recall supporting facts and details
- ☑ Arrange events in sequential order
- ☐ Follow written directions
- ☐ Describe the setting of a story (time and place)

Objective 3:

- ☐ Identify the stated or paraphrased main idea of a selection
- ☑ Identify the best summary of a selection

Objective 4:

- ☑ Identify cause and effect relationships
- ☐ Predict probable future outcomes

Objective 5:

- ☑ Understand the feelings and emotions of characters

Objective 6:

- ☑ Distinguish between fact and nonfact

Who was Sojourner Truth?

Life as a Slave

Isabella's parents were slaves in New York. When she was born in 1797, her parents wanted to keep her. Their <u>master</u> sold their first eight children to other slave owners. However, he let Isabella stay with her parents. In 1800 her <u>master</u> died. He left his land and slaves to his son, Charles. Charles gave land to Isabella and her parents. They grew their own crops on the land.

In 1808, Charles died. John Nealy, a cruel man, bought Isabella. He did not treat her nicely. Her father asked a local man to buy her from Nealy. The man bought Isabella and his family treated her well. Sadly, they sold her to John Dumont in 1810.

Freedom Comes

In 1824, a new law changed Isabella's life. Slave owners had to free slaves born before July 4, 1799. Isabella's owners said she could be free. Then later they tried to keep her. Isabella ran away. A kind family protected her and gave her shelter and food. She stayed and worked with them as a free woman.

Isabella's son was also a slave, but he belonged to a different <u>master</u>. With help from other people, Isabella sued her son's owner. It <u>stunned</u> many people when she won the case. Her son's owners had to free him. No black woman had ever won a lawsuit against a slave owner.

Living in New York City

In 1829, Isabella and her son moved to New York City. She worked for a church and taught work skills to young people. They needed these skills to find jobs. Isabella did good work, but she was unhappy. She did not think New York City was a good place for her son. In 1843, Isabella and her son left the city.

A Changed Name

After leaving New York City, Isabella changed her name to Sojourner Truth. Sojourner means traveler. She wanted to travel around the country and help people. She chose Truth as a last name. She believed in truth and honesty. Both names seemed to fit her.

Sojourner Truth

Sojourner traveled and taught about kindness and truth. She met important people like William Lloyd Garrison. He was an <u>abolitionist</u>. This was a person who wanted to get rid of slavery. She also met a black man named Frederick Douglass, another <u>abolitionist</u>. Sojourner talked to them about slavery. Soon she also began to speak out against slavery. She became one of the most popular speakers in the country.

The End of a Great Life

Sojourner worked for many years. She taught former slaves and worked at a hospital for former slaves. In 1878, she stopped traveling. She was very old. Her health was not good.

Sojourner Truth died on November 26, 1883. She was a remarkable woman. She had done many great things for the country. Today, people still learn about her work. Truly, she was a "traveler for truth."

Unfamiliar Words (1)

1. In this passage, the word <u>master</u> means—

   ◯ helper
   ◯ slave
   ◯ owner
   ◯ parent

Prefixes/Suffixes

2. What does the word <u>abolitionist</u> mean in this passage?

   ◯ A person who owned slaves
   ◯ A person who sold slaves
   ◯ A person who wanted to get rid of slavery
   ◯ A person who had been a slave

Prefixes/Suffixes (1)

3. In this passage, the word <u>stunned</u> means—

   ◯ surprised
   ◯ free
   ◯ sad
   ◯ protected

Facts/Details (2)

4. When did Isabella move to New York City?

   ◯ 1797
   ◯ 1808
   ◯ 1824
   ◯ 1829

Sequential Order (2)

5. Isabella changed her name—

   ○ before moving to New York City
   ○ after leaving New York City
   ○ right after she became free
   ○ after she met William Lloyd Garrison

Best Summary (3)

6. Which is the best summary of this passage?

   ○ Isabella's parents fought hard to protect the only child they could keep.
   ○ Slave masters were cruel people and did not want to free their slaves.
   ○ Isabella moved to New York and taught young people.
   ○ Sojourner Truth was once a slave, but she gained her freedom and helped many people.

Cause/Effect (4)

7. Isabella left New York City because—

   ○ she had finished all the work she could do
   ○ she wanted to work with William Lloyd Garrison
   ○ she thought the city was a bad place for her son
   ○ she could not find a job there

Feelings/Emotions of Characters (5)

8. From information in the passage, Sojourner Truth seemed to be—

   ○ scared
   ○ helpful
   ○ mean
   ○ angry

Fact/Nonfact (6)

9. Which is an OPINION in this passage?

   ○ Sojourner Truth was a remarkable woman.
   ○ Sojourner Truth was once a slave.
   ○ Isabella had more than one master.
   ○ Sojourner Truth taught former slaves.

Fact/Nonfact (6)

10. Which is a FACT in this passage?

   ○ Sojourner Truth was always kind and honest.
   ○ Sojourner Truth was the most popular speaker in the country.
   ○ Sojourner Truth made speeches against slavery.
   ○ Sojourner Truth was very happy in New York City.

Title: Food Named After People

Number of Words: 348

Objectives/Instructional Targets:

Objective 1:

☑ Use knowledge of the meanings of prefixes and suffixes to determine word meanings

☑ Use context clues to determine the meanings of unfamiliar words

☐ Use context clues to determine the meanings of specialized/technical terms

Objective 2:

☑ Recall supporting facts and details

☑ Arrange events in sequential order

☐ Follow written directions

☐ Describe the setting of a story (time and place)

Objective 3:

☐ Identify the stated or paraphrased main idea of a selection

☑ Identify the best summary of a selection

Objective 4:

☑ Identify cause and effect relationships

☐ Predict probable future outcomes

Objective 5:

☑ Understand the feelings and emotions of characters

Objective 6:

☑ Distinguish between fact and nonfact

Food Named After People

Where do foods get their names? Some foods get their names from the people who invented them. Other foods get their names from people who liked to eat them.

The sandwich is a common lunch food. It took its name from James Montague. Montague lived in the 1700s. He was the Fourth Earl of Sandwich. Sandwich was an area in England. Montague liked to play cards very much. One day, he was playing in a very exciting card game. It was so exciting that he didn't want to leave the table and eat his lunch. He told his servant to bring him some meat between two slices of bread. According to the story, Montague thought he discovered a <u>convenient</u> way to eat a meal. He could eat his dinner and go on with his card game at the same time! That was the beginning of the sandwich. If you like sandwiches, you can thank John Montague for his invention.

Do you ever eat toast for breakfast? Have you ever eaten Melba toast? Melba toast is a very thin slice of bread that has been toasted for a long time. It is very <u>crisp</u> and dry. Melba toast came from an accident. Nellie Melba was a famous singer at a hotel in London. One day she ordered regular toast. The chef made a mistake and cut the bread much thinner than usual. When he toasted the bread, it became very <u>crisp</u> and dry. A waiter took the toast to Nellie Melba before the chef could stop him. The chef was upset by his <u>blunder.</u> He went to apologize to Ms. Melba. To his surprise, she was eating his "mistake." She told the chef that the toast tasted wonderful. The chef began serving the thin, dark toast to other guests at the hotel. He gave the new item a very special name. He called it Melba toast. Today, you can buy Melba toast in most grocery stores.

It's fun to find out how foods got their names! Can you think of any other foods that take their names from people?

Unfamiliar Words (1)

1. In this passage, the word <u>convenient</u> means—

   ○ hard
   ○ silly
   ○ long
   ○ easy

Unfamiliar Words (1)

2. What does the word <u>crisp</u> mean in this passage?

   ○ Hard
   ○ Soft
   ○ Thick
   ○ Sliced

Prefixes/Suffixes (1)

3. In this passage, the word <u>blunder</u> means—

   ○ waiter
   ○ surprise
   ○ mistake
   ○ hotel

Facts/Details (2)

4. The first sandwich was eaten at a—

   ○ hotel
   ○ concert
   ○ card game
   ○ grocery store

Sequential Order (2)

5. The chef served thin, dark toast to other guests—

   ○ after Nellie said it tasted wonderful
   ○ before he apologized to Nellie
   ○ just before Nellie ate her toast
   ○ before Nellie ordered toast

Best Summary (3)

6. Which is the best summary of this passage?

   ○ Foods get their names in many funny ways.
   ○ Sandwiches are very easy to eat.
   ○ Melba toast was caused by a chef's accident.
   ○ Some foods, like sandwiches and Melba toast, have been named for people.

Cause/Effect (4)

7. John Montague asked for meat between two slices of bread because—

- ⬭ his servant did not know how to make other food
- ⬭ he wanted something he could eat at the card table
- ⬭ his servant had to make his lunch quickly
- ⬭ this was his favorite lunch

Feelings/Emotions of Characters (5)

8. When the waiter served burned toast to Nellie, how did the chef feel?

- ⬭ Angry
- ⬭ Proud
- ⬭ Ashamed
- ⬭ Surprised

Fact/Nonfact (6)

9. Which is an OPINION in this passage?

- ⬭ It's fun to find out how foods got their names.
- ⬭ John Montague was the Fourth Earl of Sandwich.
- ⬭ The chef burned Nellie's toast on purpose.
- ⬭ John Montague liked sandwiches better than any other food.

Fact/Nonfact (6)

10. Which is a FACT in this passage?

- ⬭ John Montague played cards better than anyone else.
- ⬭ Melba toast is ordered more often than other kinds of toast.
- ⬭ Sandwich was an area in England.
- ⬭ Melba toast tastes wonderful.

Title: Why Crabs Dig in the Sand

Number of Words: 487

Objectives/Instructional Targets:

Objective 1:

- ☑ Use knowledge of the meanings of prefixes and suffixes to determine word meanings
- ☑ Use context clues to determine the meanings of unfamiliar words
- ☐ Use context clues to determine the meanings of specialized/technical terms

Objective 2:

- ☐ Recall supporting facts and details
- ☑ Arrange events in sequential order
- ☐ Follow written directions
- ☑ Describe the setting of a story (time and place)

Objective 3:

- ☐ Identify the stated or paraphrased main idea of a selection
- ☑ Identify the best summary of a selection

Objective 4:

- ☑ Identify cause and effect relationships
- ☐ Predict probable future outcomes

Objective 5:

- ☑ Understand the feelings and emotions of characters

Objective 6:

- ☐ Distinguish between fact and nonfact

Why Crabs Dig in the Sand

One misty evening, Tommy and Grandfather were walking along the beach. The weather was <u>dreary</u>, but Tommy had begged his grandfather to walk with him. He wanted Grandfather to tell him the story about the crabs on the beach. He had heard the story over and over. He knew it by heart, but that didn't matter. Tommy wanted to hear it again.

Grandfather always began in the same way. He would describe the days when there were kings and knights. He told about their adventures and daring deeds. When Grandfather talked about their castles, he gave every <u>detail</u>. It was as if he had lived during that time. After he had set the scene, Grandfather grew quiet and looked at Tommy. Then the real story began.

There once was a king who ruled over many people. He was rich and powerful. He <u>conquered</u> many of the richest nations and took their treasures. He used the treasures to help people. Strangely, though, the king never took the treasures back to his kingdom. He did not want his people to see the treasures. He did not want them to become greedy. The king always buried the treasures on a beach near the sea. Only his most faithful knights knew about the buried treasure. Even the knights did not know exactly where to find the king's treasures.

The king was getting older. Late one spring, he became very sick. He did not think he would live much longer. He called his knights together. He told them that they could have the buried treasures if they promised to protect his kingdom forever. They could never let an enemy touch his kingdom or the riches he left behind.

After their king died, the knights were very sad. Even though they were sad, they went to search for the buried treasures. They dug for years and years on all the beaches. They did not know that someone else wanted the treasures, too.

The Lord of the Sea had watched their king for years. He wanted the treasures, too. Each day the Lord of the Sea sent his tide onto the beaches. Each day the tide took another layer of sand from the beach. The tide worked hard for the Lord of the Sea, but it could never uncover the treasures.

After working and working, the knights finally found one of the treasures. The Lord of the Sea feared they might find more. He wanted to stop them. He angrily turned all the knights into small crabs. But the knights had always been <u>loyal</u> to their king and his kingdom. They kept digging and digging in the sand.

"And that, Tommy, is why the little crabs still dig in the sand today," Grandfather said.

Tommy smiled and looked down at the sand...and the little crabs were still digging.

Unfamiliar Words (1)

1. In this passage, the word <u>dreary</u> means—

   ○ bright and cheery
   ○ sunny and warm
   ○ hot and windy
   ○ damp and cloudy

Unfamiliar Words (1)

2. What does the word <u>detail</u> mean in this passage?

   ○ Piece of information
   ○ Story
   ○ Adventure
   ○ Real story

Prefixes/Suffixes

3. In this passage, the word <u>conquered</u> means—

   ○ returned
   ○ lost
   ○ defeated
   ○ hid

Unfamiliar Words (1)

4. In this passage, the word <u>loyal</u> means—

   ○ greedy
   ○ angry
   ○ faithful
   ○ happy

Sequential Order (2)

5. What happened right after the king died?

   ○ The knights decided to give away his treasures.
   ○ The knights went to search for the buried treasures.
   ○ The knights buried the treasures in another place.
   ○ The knights fought a battle against the Lord of the Sea.

Setting of Story (2)

6. Where is Grandfather when he tells Tommy this story?

- ⬭ In Tommy's house
- ⬭ At the king's castle
- ⬭ At his house
- ⬭ On the beach

Best Summary (3)

7. Which is the best summary of this story?

- ⬭ A grandfather and grandson walk on a beach and find tiny crabs.
- ⬭ A boy asks his grandfather to explain why crabs dig in the sand.
- ⬭ A grandfather's story gives a make-believe explanation of why crabs dig in the sand.
- ⬭ A king orders his knights to bury his treasure in the sand.

Cause/Effect (4)

8. The king hid all his treasures because he—

- ⬭ wanted his knights to look for the treasures
- ⬭ did not want people in his kingdom to become greedy
- ⬭ knew the Lord of the Sea wanted to steal them
- ⬭ did not want Tommy and his grandfather to find them

Feelings/Emotions of Characters (5)

9. How did Tommy feel about hearing his grandfather's story?

- ⬭ Uninterested
- ⬭ Bored
- ⬭ Nervous
- ⬭ Eager

Feelings/Emotions of Characters (5)

10. How did Grandfather probably feel about telling his story?

- ⬭ Pleased
- ⬭ Angry
- ⬭ Nervous
- ⬭ Useless

Title: A New Way to Study

Number of Words: 500

Objectives/Instructional Targets:

Objective 1:

- ☑ Use knowledge of the meanings of prefixes and suffixes to determine word meanings
- ☑ Use context clues to determine the meanings of unfamiliar words
- ☐ Use context clues to determine the meanings of specialized/technical terms

Objective 2:

- ☐ Recall supporting facts and details
- ☑ Arrange events in sequential order
- ☑ Follow written directions
- ☐ Describe the setting of a story (time and place)

Objective 3:

- ☑ Identify the stated or paraphrased main idea of a selection
- ☐ Identify the best summary of a selection

Objective 4:

- ☑ Identify cause and effect relationships
- ☑ Predict probable future outcomes

Objective 5:

- ☐ Understand the feelings and emotions of characters

Objective 6:

- ☑ Distinguish between fact and nonfact

A New Way to Study

There are many good ways to study. You may already know some of them. One easy and useful way to study is called SQ3R. SQ3R stands for five simple steps—

- <u>Survey</u>
- Question
- Read
- <u>Recite</u>
- Review

You can use SQ3R for almost any school lesson. Once you learn and use the five steps, you can do any assignment in a planned way. SQ3R is an easy way to learn and remember what you need to know.

How to Use SQ3R

SQ3R includes five steps for studying. Always follow these five steps in the same order.

1. <u>Survey</u> the lesson or information that you want to study. Look over the whole assignment before you begin. Try to get a good idea about the work you must do. If it is a reading assignment, look over the

whole passage. How is the reading organized? Look at the beginning, middle, and end. Pay attention to pictures, graphs, and charts. Are there questions at the end? If there are, you should read them, too. The questions can show you what the lesson is about. If it is a writing assignment, do the same thing. Look at the questions you must answer. Figure out what you will need to know at the end.

2. Next, ask yourself some questions about your assignment. Make up questions from the headings, titles, and pictures. For example, you could make up a question about the passage you are reading now— "How do I use the SQ3R study method?" Write your questions on paper. Use your questions to guide your reading and studying. Your teacher may give you questions. You should use these to guide your reading, too. Remember, though, that it is important to make up your own questions. This helps you learn more.

3. The next step is to read (or write) your assignment. Think about the questions from step two. Use the questions to guide your work. Look for the answers to the questions.

4. Now it is time to <u>recite</u>. After you finish the third step, answer the questions from step two. If you have written answers, read over your work. Make sure you have answered what was asked. You

can also ask someone else to ask you questions. Your mom, dad, or older brother or sister can ask questions about your work. This is a good time to summarize the work. Can you explain the main ideas in a few words?

5. Finally, look over your work one last time. What was it about? Did you finish the whole assignment? Did you answer all your questions? What did you learn?

Why Use SQ3R

SQ3R can help you with any assignment. It will also help you be a more independent reader and learner. You will feel good about working on your own. You will be learning how to direct your own school work. And, you will probably become a better student. SQ3R is a study method you can use throughout your life.

Unfamiliar Words (1)

1. In this passage, the word survey means—

    ○ finish
    ○ write
    ○ look over
    ○ remember

Unfamiliar Words (1)

2. What does the word recite mean in this passage?

    ○ Give the answers
    ○ Stop studying
    ○ Write or read
    ○ Help someone

Prefixes/Suffixes (1)

3. In this passage, the word summarize means—

    ○ use many details
    ○ ask for help
    ○ present main ideas in a few words
    ○ take a rest

Prefixes/Suffixes (1)

4. In this passage, the word independent means—

    ○ needing help from others
    ○ able to work alone
    ○ slow and careful
    ○ interesting

Sequential Order (2)

5. Which is the last step of SQ3R?

- ⬭ Explain each answer to your parents
- ⬭ Look at how the lesson is organized
- ⬭ Write your questions on paper
- ⬭ Look over your work one last time

Following Directions (2)

6. You should look over the questions before you begin an assignment because—

- ⬭ this is the only way to answer them
- ⬭ they can show you what the lesson is about
- ⬭ this will make you more independent
- ⬭ this is the fastest way to work

Stated/Paraphrased Main Idea (3)

7. This passage is mostly about—

- ⬭ the best way to get better grades
- ⬭ answering questions correctly
- ⬭ how to use SQ3R to study
- ⬭ how to improve your grades

Cause/Effect (4)

8. According to the passage, if you make up your own questions, then you will—

- ⬭ learn more
- ⬭ waste too much time
- ⬭ make your teacher happy
- ⬭ know what the assignment is

Predicting Outcomes (4)

9. What will probably happen if you learn and use SQ3R?

- ⬭ You will earn all A's on your report card.
- ⬭ Your teacher will give you more work.
- ⬭ You will become a better student.
- ⬭ You will spend less time on school work.

Fact/Nonfact (6)

10. Which is an OPINION in this passage?

- ⬭ The first step in SQ3R is to survey.
- ⬭ SQ3R is an easy way to study.
- ⬭ Everyone should study in the same way.
- ⬭ SQ3R has five steps.

Title: Fly Away Home

Number of Words: 491

Objectives/Instructional Targets:

Objective 1:

- ☑ Use knowledge of the meanings of prefixes and suffixes to determine word meanings
- ☑ Use context clues to determine the meanings of unfamiliar words
- ☑ Use context clues to determine the meanings of specialized/technical terms

Objective 2:

- ☑ Recall supporting facts and details
- ☑ Arrange events in sequential order
- ☐ Follow written directions
- ☐ Describe the setting of a story (time and place)

Objective 3:

- ☐ Identify the stated or paraphrased main idea of a selection
- ☑ Identify the best summary of a selection

Objective 4:

- ☑ Identify cause and effect relationships
- ☐ Predict probable future outcomes

Objective 5:

- ☐ Understand the feelings and emotions of characters

Objective 6:

- ☑ Distinguish between fact and nonfact

Fly Away Home

In China people call them "flower ladies." People in Europe may call them "little fatties." You may know them as "ladybugs" or "lady beetles." Whatever we call them, these small, round insects are important friends to people around the world.

All Kinds of Ladybugs

Ladybugs are small beetles. Like all beetles, they are insects. There are more than 3,000 kinds of ladybugs in the world. In this country, there are more than 100 kinds. Each kind is a little different from the others.

All ladybugs are small. The largest kind is no more than $^1/_3$ to $^1/_2$ inch long. Some kinds are even smaller than that—maybe less than $^1/_{10}$ inch long.

You may be most familiar with the small, red ladybug with seven black spots. Ladybugs actually come in many colors, like orange, yellow, and black. Some have no markings on their outer, colored shells. However, most varieties have black spots or patches. Some ladybugs have two spots. Others have five or seven spots. Some of these little beetles have more than 20 spots on their backs!

All ladybugs have hard shells on their bodies. The shells are called elytra. These outer coverings look like wings, but they are not. The elytra cover and protect the ladybug's "flying" wings. The flying wings are much longer and thinner than the hard shells. When a ladybug wants to fly, it lifts the hard shells and spreads its wings. Then it takes off!

Warning: Stay Away

Like most animals, the ladybug must protect itself from enemies. Its first defense is its color. Its color can blend in with its surroundings. This makes the ladybug hard to see. The colorful markings also warn enemies like ants and birds that ladybugs taste bad. A ladybug protects itself in another way, too. It can release a bad-smelling liquid through its legs. This is called reflex bleeding. The bad smell tells the ladybug's enemies to "stay away."

A Ladybug's Diet

A ladybug is no "lady" when it comes to eating. Every ladybug has a huge appetite. One adult ladybug may eat more than 50 insects in one day! Ladybugs eat many kinds of insects, including spider mites and scale ladybugs. Its favorite meal is the aphid.

The ladybug's diet makes it a friend to farmers and gardeners. It eats many of the insects that destroy crops. For example, aphids, or plant lice, live on plants and suck food from them. This can kill the plants. To protect their plants, many growers let ladybugs loose in their fields or gardens. The ladybugs eat the unwanted guests. In some places, people even have "ladybug farms." They raise ladybugs and sell them to growers who need them.

Ladybugs are colorful and helpful members of the insect world. If one lands on your shoulder, look at it carefully. You might also say, "Thanks for your help, little fatty."

Unfamiliar Words (1)

1. In this passage, the word varieties means—

   ⬭ insects
   ⬭ ladybugs
   ⬭ spots
   ⬭ different kinds

Specialized/Technical Terms (1)

2. What does the word elytra mean in this passage?

   ⬭ A ladybug's true wings
   ⬭ The spots on a ladybug's back
   ⬭ Outer coverings that protect a ladybug's wings
   ⬭ A ladybug's enemy

Prefixes/Suffixes (1)

3. In this passage, the word defense means—

   ⬭ color
   ⬭ surroundings
   ⬭ protection
   ⬭ markings

Specialized/Technical Terms (1)

4. In this passage, the word aphids means—

   ⬭ plant lice
   ⬭ farmers and gardeners
   ⬭ ladybug farms
   ⬭ unwanted insects

Facts/Details (2)

5. How many kinds of ladybugs are in the world?

- ⬭ 20
- ⬭ 50
- ⬭ 100
- ⬭ 3,000

Facts/Details (2)

6. Reflex bleeding is how a ladybug—

- ⬭ blends in with its surroundings
- ⬭ makes colorful markings
- ⬭ makes a smell to keep its enemies away
- ⬭ lifts its wings

Sequential Order (2)

7. In order to fly, a ladybug must first—

- ⬭ release liquid from its legs
- ⬭ lift its hard shell
- ⬭ have at least seven spots
- ⬭ protect itself from enemies

Best Summary (3)

8. Which is the best summary of the sixth paragraph?

- ⬭ Ladybugs can blend in with their surroundings.
- ⬭ Ladybugs have several ways to protect themselves from their enemies.
- ⬭ Ladybugs are interesting and useful insects.
- ⬭ Ants and birds do not like the taste of ladybugs.

Cause/Effect (4)

9. Some farmers release ladybugs in their fields in order to—

- ⬭ give ladybugs a good diet
- ⬭ raise ladybugs and sell them to other farmers
- ⬭ make the surroundings more beautiful and interesting
- ⬭ get rid of insects that destroy crops

Fact/Nonfact (6)

10. Which is a FACT in this passage?

- ⬭ In China, people call ladybugs "little fatties."
- ⬭ Ladybugs can come in many different colors.
- ⬭ Ladybugs are the most important insects in the world.
- ⬭ Everyone in the world likes to look at ladybugs.

Title: What kind of pet is it?

Number of Words: 391

Objectives/Instructional Targets:

Objective 1:

☑ Use knowledge of the meanings of prefixes and suffixes to determine word meanings
☑ Use context clues to determine the meanings of unfamiliar words
☑ Use context clues to determine the meanings of specialized/technical terms

Objective 2:

☑ Recall supporting facts and details
☐ Arrange events in sequential order
☑ Follow written directions
☐ Describe the setting of a story (time and place)

Objective 3:

☑ Identify the stated or paraphrased main idea of a selection
☐ Identify the best summary of a selection

Objective 4:

☑ Identify cause and effect relationships
☐ Predict probable future outcomes

Objective 5:

☐ Understand the feelings and emotions of characters

Objective 6:

☑ Distinguish between fact and nonfact

What kind of pet is it?

In the wild they live in <u>colonies</u> or groups. They get very lonely without company, so you should have two. They are friendly, frisky, and furry. They are also curious and clean. And they seldom bite! These mammals are about three to four inches long (including their tails). They weigh between two and three ounces. Can you guess which pets are being described?

If you guessed gerbils, you are right! As pets, gerbils are easy to care for. They take up little space and are not very smelly. If you want indoor cuddly companions, these guys may be just the ticket.

Housing gerbils is easy. Their <u>native habitats</u> are the deserts of Asia and North Africa. This explains their burrowing habit. It is best to give them a gerbilarium. A regular 10-gallon aquarium is fine for two. Do not place it in direct sunlight. Gerbils can be overcome by the heat. Fill their home with several inches of <u>bedding</u>. Sawdust, wood chips, or white paper torn into small pieces are good choices. (Do not use newspaper. The ink could poison your new friends!) The gerbils will do the rest. They will shred, pile, and constantly rearrange their home.

Next you need a small, heavy bowl for food. You also will need a hanging water bottle. These busy little creatures will overturn anything that moves. Change the bedding about every two weeks. At the same time rinse out the gerbilarium with a mild soap. Replace the water daily. This will keep it fresh.

Toys please your perky pets and make them more fun to watch. Give them wood to gnaw and climb or a small piece of cloth to shred. For hiding and sleeping, they also enjoy cardboard centers from paper towels. Don't forget to give them an exercise wheel. Do not give them plastic. They will chew and swallow the plastic.

Gerbils do not eat meat. It is easy to supply their <u>vegetarian</u> diet. You can buy a prepackaged mix at the pet store. For a special treat, give them carrots, cheese, apples, or even wild dandelions once in a while.

Now relax and enjoy your pets. Be gentle and give them the attention they need. The payoff will be the trust and friendship of a gerbil's lifetime.

Unfamiliar Words (1)

1. In this passage, the word <u>colonies</u> means—

   ◯ small mammals
   ◯ groups of animals that live together
   ◯ pets that live in cages
   ◯ gerbils kept as pets

Specialized/Technical Terms (1)

2. What does the term <u>native habitats</u> mean in this passage?

   ◯ Gerbil cages
   ◯ Deserts in Asia
   ◯ Natural living areas
   ◯ Homes for pets

Prefixes/Suffixes (1)

3. In this passage, the word <u>bedding</u> means—

   ◯ a 10-gallon aquarium
   ◯ old newspaper
   ◯ material used to make a bed
   ◯ a place to sleep

Prefixes/Suffixes (1)

4. What does the word <u>vegetarian</u> mean in this passage?

   ◯ Containing only meat
   ◯ Containing only vegetables
   ◯ A special treat
   ◯ Containing pet food

Facts/Details (2)

5. Which of the following is a good choice for a gerbil's bedding?

   ◯ Dandelions
   ◯ Newpaper
   ◯ Sand
   ◯ Wood Chips

Following Directions (2)

6. Since gerbils like to chew on things, you should—

   ◯ give them only soft foods
   ◯ use plastic toys they cannot destroy
   ◯ clean their houses every two weeks
   ◯ give them wood to chew

Stated/Paraphrased Main Idea (3)

7. The fifth paragraph is mostly about—

- good toys for gerbils
- why gerbils need to exercise
- watching gerbils play
- why gerbils like to hide

Cause/Effect (4)

8. A gerbil's house should not be in direct sunlight because—

- gerbils cannot sleep in the sunlight
- gerbils chew more when in direct sunlight
- too much heat can hurt gerbils
- the gerbil's food will spoil

Fact/Nonfact (6)

9. Which is an OPINION in this passage?

- Gerbils need plastic toys.
- Gerbils are easy to care for.
- Gerbils are really desert animals.
- Gerbils need fresh water every day.

Title: First-Class Snack

Number of Words: 308

Objectives/Instructional Targets:

Objective 1:

- ☑ Use knowledge of the meanings of prefixes and suffixes to determine word meanings
- ☑ Use context clues to determine the meanings of unfamiliar words
- ☑ Use context clues to determine the meanings of specialized/technical terms

Objective 2:

- ☐ Recall supporting facts and details
- ☑ Arrange events in sequential order
- ☑ Follow written directions
- ☐ Describe the setting of a story (time and place)

Objective 3:

- ☑ Identify the stated or paraphrased main idea of a selection
- ☐ Identify the best summary of a selection

Objective 4:

- ☐ Identify cause and effect relationships
- ☐ Predict probable future outcomes

Objective 5:

- ☐ Understand the feelings and emotions of characters

Objective 6:

- ☑ Distinguish between fact and nonfact

First-Class Snack

What do we put in envelopes? Important papers, bills, cards, and letters, to name just a few things. People use envelopes to keep what is inside secret, so that only the person who receives the envelope can read the message.

Now you can make your own envelope—and eat it, too! This recipe uses broccoli and cheddar cheese, but you can use something different, such as apples, cherries, blueberries, peaches, asparagus, mushrooms, or another fruit or vegetable. Have fun making your <u>edible</u> envelope—but don't mail it!

You need:

- pie dough (buy the kind that is already mixed—it is easier!)
- a head of fresh broccoli
- your favorite cheese

To prepare the filling, wash the broccoli well and cut the buds at the top into one-inch pieces. Cut up enough to fill two cups (this will fill four envelopes). Grate one cup of cheese.

Roll out the dough (not too thin) on a floured board. Cut a six-inch square out of the dough, then put about $1/2$ cup of broccoli in the middle of the square and sprinkle $1/4$ cup of cheese on the top.

To make your envelope, fold the two side corners, then fold the bottom corner over them. Finally, fold the top down. Make sure there are no <u>gaps</u> where the filling could leak out of your envelope.

Use a small piece of dough to make a seal for your envelope. Then use a spatula to put the envelope on an <u>ungreased</u> cookie sheet. Repeat this <u>procedure</u> for the other three envelopes.

Bake at 375° for about 20 minutes or until the top turns brown. Take the envelopes out of the oven and let them cool on a rack until they are ready to serve. Fruit envelopes taste delicious when served with ice cream.

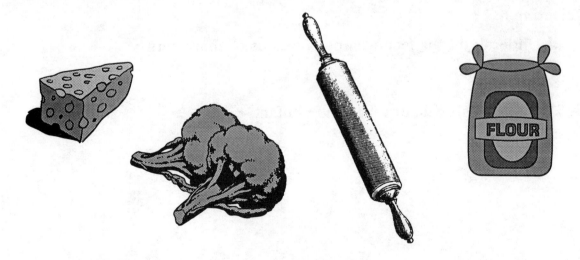

Unfamiliar Words (1)

1. In this passage, what does the word <u>edible</u> mean?

   ⬭ Filled with fruit
   ⬭ Can be eaten
   ⬭ Made of dough
   ⬭ Different

Unfamiliar Words (1)

2. What does the word <u>gaps</u> mean in this passage?

   ⬭ Openings
   ⬭ Bottoms
   ⬭ Corners
   ⬭ Tops

Prefixes/Suffixes (1)

3. In this passage, the word <u>ungreased</u> means—

   ⬭ empty
   ⬭ not baked
   ⬭ not greased
   ⬭ small

Specialized/Technical Terms (1)

4. In this passage, the word <u>procedure</u> means—

   ⬭ message
   ⬭ way of doing something
   ⬭ seal for an envelope
   ⬭ folding

Sequential Order (2)

5. What should you do right after folding down the top corner of the dough envelope?

   ○ Make a seal for the envelope
   ○ Stuff the envelope with fruit
   ○ Bake the envelope on a cookie sheet
   ○ Check for gaps that could leak

Following Directions (2)

6. When making these snacks, you should—

   ○ only use a cheese or fruit filling
   ○ let them cool after baking
   ○ make another set of snacks
   ○ eat them as soon as possible

Stated/Paraphrased Main Idea (3)

7. This passage is mostly about—

   ○ why you should eat vegetables and fruits
   ○ choosing the right fillings for the snacks
   ○ making envelope-shaped snacks
   ○ how to mail something in an envelope

Fact/Nonfact (6)

8. Which is an OPINION in this passage?

   ○ Fruit envelopes taste delicious when served with ice cream.
   ○ Papers, bills, and letters can be kept in real envelopes.
   ○ Pie dough is used to make this snack.
   ○ You can mail this envelope snack to people.

Title: How much do you know about the bluebonnet?

Number of Words: 453

Objectives/Instructional Targets:

Objective 1:

- ☑ Use knowledge of the meanings of prefixes and suffixes to determine word meanings
- ☑ Use context clues to determine the meanings of unfamiliar words
- ☑ Use context clues to determine the meanings of specialized/technical terms

Objective 2:

- ☑ Recall supporting facts and details
- ☐ Arrange events in sequential order
- ☑ Follow written directions
- ☐ Describe the setting of a story (time and place)

Objective 3:

- ☑ Identify the stated or paraphrased main idea of a selection
- ☐ Identify the best summary of a selection

Objective 4:

- ☑ Identify cause and effect relationships
- ☐ Predict probable future outcomes

Objective 5:

- ☐ Understand the feelings and emotions of characters

Objective 6:

- ☑ Distinguish between fact and nonfact

How much do you know about the bluebonnet?

Of course, you know that the bluebonnet is the state flower of Texas. The bluebonnet became the state flower on March 7, 1901. At that time, only one kind of bluebonnet became the state flower. Other <u>varieties</u> of bluebonnets were not included. In 1971, a new state law was passed. This law said that any flower in the bluebonnet family was the state flower.

What's in a name?

In the past, the bluebonnet has had different names. In some places, people called it the wolf flower. Other people called it buffalo clover. One of its most unusual names was "el conejo." This means "the rabbit." It is a Spanish <u>phrase.</u> Why did people give this name to a bluebonnet? They could see a rabbit in each tiny flower. Take a close look at the next bluebonnet you see. Maybe you will see a rabbit, too.

Today, nearly everyone calls the flower a bluebonnet. How did the flower earn that name? The pioneer women in Texas often wore bright hats to block the sun. These were called sunbonnets. Many pioneers thought the flowers looked like the women's sunbonnets. This is how the flower earned its most popular name.

Scientists give each kind of plant a special name, too. Every kind of plant has a different name. In a way, the name explains why each plant is <u>unlike</u> any other plant. A plant's <u>scientific</u> name is always in Latin, a very old language. The bluebonnet's <u>scientific</u> name is *Lupinus texensis.*

Looking at Bluebonnets

Most bluebonnet plants are from nine to twelve inches tall. The small plants first appear in early spring. They grow in small groups, or clumps, along the state's highways and roads. The first flowers usually appear in March. Most of the flowers look like tall towers of blue and white, but some of the flowers may be all white or pink and white. The plant's leaves and stems feel "hairy." The flowers have a nice, sweet <u>fragrance,</u> or smell.

Growing Bluebonnets

Bluebonnets are really wildflowers. This means they grow "on their own" in nature. However, you can plant bluebonnets in a yard, garden, or field.

Plant bluebonnet seeds in the fall. Do not plant them very deep in the soil. Scatter the seed in a place that gets lots of sun in the spring. Use a rake to spread a thin layer of dirt over the seeds. In the spring, you should have your first crop of bluebonnets.

If you want more and more bluebonnets each year, it is best not to pick the flowers. Let the flowers die on the plants. The dying flowers will drop their seeds in the soil. Next year, you will have even more lovely bluebonnets to enjoy!

Unfamiliar Words (1)

1. What does the word <u>varieties</u> mean in this passage?

   ◯ Flowers
   ◯ Kinds
   ◯ Leaves
   ◯ States

Unfamiliar Words (1)

2. In this passage, the word <u>phrase</u> means—

   ◯ tiny flowers
   ◯ bluebonnet
   ◯ group of words
   ◯ wolf flower

Specialized/Technical Words (1)

3. In this passage, the word <u>scientific</u> means—

   ◯ like a flower
   ◯ not like science
   ◯ belonging to plants
   ◯ from science

Prefixes/Suffixes (1)

4. In this passage, what does the word <u>unlike</u> mean?

   ◯ Special
   ◯ Very old
   ◯ Not the same as
   ◯ Not in Texas

Unfamiliar Words (1)

5. In this passage, the word <u>fragance</u> means—

   ○ smell
   ○ stem
   ○ color
   ○ soil

Facts/Details (2)

6. When should bluebonnet seeds be planted?

   ○ Early spring
   ○ March
   ○ Late summer
   ○ Fall

Following Directions (2)

7. Bluebonnet seeds should be planted—

   ○ deep in the soil
   ○ along the highway
   ○ in sunny places
   ○ away from other flowers

Stated/Paraphrased Main Idea (3)

8. The second paragraph is mostly about—

   ○ the correct name for a bluebonnet
   ○ why people call the bluebonnet "el conejo"
   ○ different names given to the bluebonnet
   ○ why the bluebonnet became the state flower

Cause/Effect (4)

9. Why should you let the flowers die on the bluebonnet plants?

   ○ So prettier flowers will grow in the spring
   ○ So the flowers will drop their seeds in the soil
   ○ So the flowers will be real wildflowers
   ○ So other flowers cannot grow

Fact/Nonfact (6)

10. Which is an OPINION in the passage?

   ○ Bluebonnets have a nice smell.
   ○ Bluebonnets were called buffalo clover.
   ○ Bluebonnet flowers can be pink and white.
   ○ The bluebonnet is the state flower of Texas.

Title: Flying a Kite—The Safe Way

Number of Words: 327

Objectives/Instructional Targets:

Objective 1:

- ☑ Use knowledge of the meanings of prefixes and suffixes to determine word meanings
- ☑ Use context clues to determine the meanings of unfamiliar words
- ☑ Use context clues to determine the meanings of specialized/technical terms

Objective 2:

- ☑ Recall supporting facts and details
- ☐ Arrange events in sequential order
- ☑ Follow written directions
- ☐ Describe the setting of a story (time and place)

Objective 3:

- ☐ Identify the stated or paraphrased main idea of a selection
- ☑ Identify the best summary of a selection

Objective 4:

- ☑ Identify cause and effect relationships
- ☐ Predict probable future outcomes

Objective 5:

- ☐ Understand the feelings and emotions of characters

Objective 6:

- ☑ Distinguish between fact and nonfact

Flying a Kite—The Safe Way

Have you ever flown a kite? Kite-flying is a great way to spend a breezy day. It's always fun to watch a colorful kite soar and dive in the sky.

Kite-flying is enjoyable, but it can also be dangerous. You should know and obey many safety rules for flying a kite. Do you know what these rules are?

Safety Rules for Kite-Flying

• Never use a kite made from any kind of metal. A kite should not have any wire or string with metal pieces. Use kites made with plastic, wooden, or paper parts.

• Use string that is clean and dry. The best kind of string to use is cotton.

• Never fly a kite if it is raining or storming. Lightning could strike the kite and injure you.

• Always fly a kite in an open area. A large field is a good place for kite-flying.

• Fly your kite far away from electric lines and towers. If a kite touches a power line or tower, it could <u>conduct</u> the electricity to your body. Of course, this is very dangerous. You could suffer many serious injuries.

• Never climb an electric pole or tower to get your kite. Again, you do not want to come near electricity. You also could fall from the pole or tower and injure yourself. If your kite lands on a pole or in its wires, leave your kite there. You should call your local power company to report the problem.

• Fly a kite away from roads and streets. This is important for both you and drivers on the road. You do not want a kite to fall on passing <u>motorists</u>. This could scare them. It is also dangerous for you to <u>retrieve</u> a fallen kite from a busy street or road.

It is important to follow these rules when you fly a kite. You want to have fun. You want to be safe, too!

Specialized/Technical Terms (1)

1. In this passage, the word <u>conduct</u> means—

   ○ remove
   ○ save
   ○ cover
   ○ carry

Prefixes/Suffixes (1)

2. What does the word <u>motorists</u> mean?

   ○ People who fly kites
   ○ People who are in the street
   ○ People who drive cars
   ○ People who follow rules

Unfamiliar Words (1)

3. In this passage, the word <u>retrieve</u> means—

   ○ go and get
   ○ drop
   ○ drive on a road
   ○ fly a kite

Facts/Details (2)

4. Which of the following is the best kind of string for a kite?

   ○ Wire
   ○ Metal
   ○ Cotton
   ○ Plastic

Following Directions (2)

5. What should you do if your kite lands on power lines?

   ○ Climb carefully and get the kite
   ○ Move to an open area
   ○ Ask a driver to help you
   ○ Leave the kite and report the problem to the power company

Following Directions (3)

6. To be safe, you should fly your kite—

   ○ near streets and roads
   ○ in a large, open area
   ○ close to local power lines
   ○ on the school grounds

Best Summary (3)

7. Which is the best summary of this passage?

- ⬭ Kite-flying is a great way to spend a breezy day.
- ⬭ Kites can be made of many different materials like wood, plastic, and paper.
- ⬭ There are important safety rules to follow when you fly a kite.
- ⬭ You should fly a kite away from power lines and roads.

Cause Effect (4)

8. You should not fly a kite in the rain or a storm because—

- ⬭ your kite could get wet
- ⬭ lightning could injure you
- ⬭ you will be scared
- ⬭ drivers will not see you

Fact/Nonfact (6)

9. Which of the following is an OPINION in this passage?

- ⬭ You should fly a kite away from power lines.
- ⬭ Kites can be made of plastic, wood, or paper.
- ⬭ If a kite touches a power line, it could conduct electricity to your body.
- ⬭ It's always fun to watch a colorful kite soar and dive in the sky.

Fact/Nonfact (6)

10. Which is a FACT in this passage?

- ⬭ Kites should not have metal parts.
- ⬭ Kite-flying is a great way to spend a breezy day.
- ⬭ Kite-flying is enjoyable.
- ⬭ Plastic is the best material for a kite.

Title: An Unusual Fish

Number of Words: 412

Objectives/Instructional Targets:

Objective 1:

- ☐ Use knowledge of the meanings of prefixes and suffixes to determine word meanings
- ☑ Use context clues to determine the meanings of unfamiliar words
- ☑ Use context clues to determine the meanings of specialized/technical terms

Objective 2:

- ☑ Recall supporting facts and details
- ☐ Arrange events in sequential order
- ☐ Follow written directions
- ☐ Describe the setting of a story (time and place)

Objective 3:

- ☑ Identify the stated or paraphrased main idea of a selection
- ☐ Identify the best summary of a selection

Objective 4:

- ☑ Identify cause and effect relationships
- ☐ Predict probable future outcomes

Objective 5:

- ☐ Understand the feelings and emotions of characters

Objective 6:

- ☑ Distinguish between fact and nonfact

An Unusual Fish

Think about a fish in the ocean. What picture comes to your mind? You probably see something that looks like a horse with a monkey's tail. You don't? Then you must not see the seahorse, a very different kind of fish.

There are more than 30 kinds of seahorses, but all of them have a similar appearance. The seahorse's head looks something like a horse's head. This fish also has a long tail that stretches down from its body. It is a prehensile tail. This means the seahorse can use the tail like a hand. With its tail, a seahorse can hold on to seaweed, other plants, or another seahorse.

The male seahorse has another interesting feature. It has a pouch, or pocket, on the front of its body. The male seahorse carries the female seahorse's eggs in the pouch. After the baby seahorses hatch, the male releases the babies from his pouch.

Seahorses come in many sizes. The smallest seahorse is about one inch long. This tiny creature lives in the Gulf of Mexico. The largest seahorse is more than one foot long. This "giant" of the seahorse family lives in the eastern Pacific Ocean.

Seahorses belong to the pipefish family. They have only one fin. It is a dorsal fin. This means the fin is on their back. Unlike most other fish, seahorses swim upright in the water. They usually move very slowly. They look like they are floating in the water.

Seahorses like to eat plankton and small fish. Plankton are very tiny animals that float in the water. The seahorse can turn each of its eyes in different directions. This is how it searches for food. It does not need to move its head. It holds on to a sea plant, searches with its eyes, and gobbles up food as it floats by.

Seahorses do not have many enemies in the sea. First of all, seahorses are bony and hard to eat. Seahorses also use camouflage to protect themselves. They can hide by changing colors. If they are near a green plant, they can match its green color. Only some kinds of crabs like to eat a seahorse meal—if they can find one!

It looks like a horse. It uses its tail like a hand. The male seahorse carries the babies in its pouch. It moves one eye to search for food. It changes colors to protect itself. Is the seahorse an unusual fish? You can decide for yourself.

Specialized/Technical Terms (1)

1. In this passage, the word prehensile means—

   ○ attached to the body
   ○ used like a hand
   ○ shaped like a horse's head
   ○ long and thin

Specialized/Technical Terms (1)

2. What does the word dorsal mean in this passage?

   ○ In a pouch
   ○ Unlike other fish
   ○ Upright in the water
   ○ On the back

Unfamiliar Words (1)

3. In this passage, the word pouch means a—

   ○ group of baby seahorses
   ○ pocket on the front of the body
   ○ male seahorse
   ○ seahorse's eggs

Specialized/Technical Terms (1)

4. In this passage, the word plankton means—

   ○ tiny animals floating in the ocean
   ○ a seahorse's eye
   ○ seaweed and other plants
   ○ a way to search for food

Unfamiliar Words (1)

5. What does the word camouflage mean in this passage?

   ○ Looking for enemies
   ○ Searching for food
   ○ Hiding by changing colors
   ○ Bony and hard to eat

Facts/Details (2)

6. According to this passage, the largest seahorse—

   ○ lives in the Gulf of Mexico
   ○ is only one inch long
   ○ is more than one foot long
   ○ does not eat plankton

Facts/Details (2)

7. A male seahorse carries the female's eggs in its—

- ⬭ head
- ⬭ pouch
- ⬭ tail
- ⬭ fin

Stated/Paraphrased Main Idea (3)

8. This passage is mostly about—

- ⬭ why seahorses have few enemies
- ⬭ how seahorses swim in the water
- ⬭ how baby seahorses are born
- ⬭ why seahorses are unusual fish

Cause/Effect (4)

9. A seahorse changes colors so it can—

- ⬭ look like other fish
- ⬭ carry eggs in its pouch
- ⬭ hide from other animals
- ⬭ eat more plankton

Fact/Nonfact (6)

10. Which is an OPINION in this passage?

- ⬭ There are more than 30 kinds of seahorses.
- ⬭ Some seahorses are only one inch long.
- ⬭ Seahorses hold on to things with their tails.
- ⬭ The seahorse is a very different kind of fish.

Title: The City Mouse and the Country Mouse

Number of Words: 500

Objectives/Instructional Targets:

Objective 1:

- ☑ Use knowledge of the meanings of prefixes and suffixes to determine word meanings
- ☑ Use context clues to determine the meanings of unfamiliar words
- ☐ Use context clues to determine the meanings of specialized/technical terms

Objective 2:

- ☐ Recall supporting facts and details
- ☑ Arrange events in sequential order
- ☐ Follow written directions
- ☑ Describe the setting of a story (time and place)

Objective 3:

- ☐ Identify the stated or paraphrased main idea of a selection
- ☐ Identify the best summary of a selection

Objective 4:

- ☑ Identify cause and effect relationships
- ☑ Predict probable future outcomes

Objective 5:

- ☑ Understand the feelings and emotions of characters

Objective 6:

- ☐ Distinguish between fact and nonfact

The City Mouse and the Country Mouse

This story is based on a fable written by Aesop, a slave in Greece. He lived more than 3,000 years ago. People enjoyed his stories then. We still enjoy them today.

Once upon a time there were two mice cousins. One lived in the country. The other lived in the city.

One day the country mouse invited the city mouse for a visit. The city mouse accepted right away. He looked forward to seeing his cousin's home in the country. He put on his best clothes and set out for the country.

When he arrived at his cousin's house, the city mouse was immediately displeased. His cousin was dressed in old jeans and a flannel shirt. Was this any way to greet a guest?

The city mouse looked around his cousin's kitchen. The country mouse had set a neat and clean table, but the food looked terrible! There was only corn, beans, and some old dried roots. The city mouse could only think about the wonderful foods back at his home.

"Is this what you eat every day, cousin?" the city mouse asked.

"Yes. It is not fancy food, but I have plenty for myself and for guests," answered the country mouse.

The city mouse shook his head. He could never live like this, he thought.

"Dear cousin," said the city mouse, "why don't we go to my home in the city. There I have enough wonderful food for both of us—cheese, fruit, carrots, breads, apples, and more."

The country mouse felt a bit sad, but he agreed to join his cousin in the city. He put on his walking shoes and they set out for the city.

The city mouse had told the truth. His table was filled with delicious foods. There were four kinds of cheese, three plates of fruits, and all sorts of bread. The country mouse could hardly believe his eyes. The two cousins sat down to enjoy their meal together.

No sooner had they taken their seats, than they heard the sound of human footsteps. They scurried to hide behind the stove. They carefully tiptoed out after the person left the kitchen. Just as they started to eat, they saw someone else standing in the doorway. Once again they ran to hide themselves.

The country mouse could feel his heart thumping against his chest. He looked at his cousin, who seemed to be shaking. He could not stand it.

"I am sorry, cousin," said the country mouse. "You were kind to invite me, but I cannot stay. I am so frightened. I would never be able to eat."

"Look at all that wonderful food," answered the city mouse. "The people will leave soon. Then we can have our feast."

"That may be true," the country mouse said, "but I am not willing to pay your price. I would rather eat my beans and roots in peace." With those words, the country mouse slipped out the door and ran home to the country.

Prefixes/Suffixes (1)

1. In this passage, the word displeased means—

   - ⬭ very glad
   - ⬭ not quick
   - ⬭ not happy
   - ⬭ very honest

Unfamiliar Words (1)

2. What does the word scurried mean in this passage?

   - ⬭ Ran quickly
   - ⬭ Hid
   - ⬭ Started to eat
   - ⬭ Listened carefully

Unfamiliar Words (1)

3. In this passage, the word slipped means—

   - ⬭ stood
   - ⬭ yelled loudly
   - ⬭ entered
   - ⬭ went quietly

Sequential Order (2)

4. What happened right after the two mice sat to eat the first time?

- ◯ They talked about the wonderful food.
- ◯ They scurried behind the stove.
- ◯ They heard human footsteps.
- ◯ They saw someone in the doorway.

Setting of Story (2)

5. Where did this story happen?

- ◯ In Greece long ago
- ◯ In the city
- ◯ In the country
- ◯ In both the city and the country

Cause/Effect (4)

6. The country mouse went back to his home because—

- ◯ he did not like the city mouse's food
- ◯ he was too scared in the city
- ◯ the city mouse asked him to leave
- ◯ his food tasted better than the city mouse's food

Predicting Outcomes (4)

7. Which of the following will the city mouse and country mouse most likely do?

- ◯ Decide to live together in the city
- ◯ Visit each other every day
- ◯ Stay in their own homes
- ◯ Trade food with each other

Feelings/Emotions of Characters (5)

8. When the city mouse saw the country mouse's food, he felt—

- ◯ excited
- ◯ silly
- ◯ disappointed
- ◯ angry

Feelings/Emotions of Characters (5)

9. When the country mouse returned to his home, he probably felt—

- ◯ frightened
- ◯ happy
- ◯ jealous
- ◯ angry

Title: The Butterfly World

Number of Words: 450

Objectives/Instructional Targets:

Objective 1:

☑ Use knowledge of the meanings of prefixes and suffixes to determine word meanings
☐ Use context clues to determine the meanings of unfamiliar words
☑ Use context clues to determine the meanings of specialized/technical terms

Objective 2:

☑ Recall supporting facts and details
☐ Arrange events in sequential order
☐ Follow written directions
☐ Describe the setting of a story (time and place)

Objective 3:

☑ Identify the stated or paraphrased main idea of a selection
☐ Identify the best summary of a selection

Objective 4:

☑ Identify cause and effect relationships
☐ Predict probable future outcomes

Objective 5:

☐ Understand the feelings and emotions of characters

Objective 6:

☑ Distinguish between fact and nonfact

The Butterfly World

There are about 20,000 kinds of butterflies in the world. Each type lives only in certain places on earth. Most people get to see only a few kinds. Just think how wonderful it would be to see all 20,000 kinds! Of course, that's impossible. You can learn about different butterflies by reading about them.

The Common Blue Butterfly

Common blue butterflies live in Europe and Asia. They like to live in cool, damp places. Some people call them "little blues," but only the male butterflies are blue. The females are brown. This butterfly is also quite small. In fact, it is the smallest butterfly in the world.

Its wingspan is only about one inch. This is the distance between the tips of the wings.

The common blue butterfly has an interesting "friendship" with ants. During the caterpillar stage, the caterpillar makes a sweet liquid. The liquid is called honeydew. Ants like to eat this sweet treat, but they do not harm the caterpillar. In fact, they protect it from its enemies. Sometimes the ants even move the caterpillar closer to their home!

The Swallowtail Butterfly

The swallowtail butterflies also live in Europe and Asia. They like to live in fields and near hills. They are bright yellow and black. There are blue and red spots on their wings. This butterfly's wingspan is about four inches.

During part of the caterpillar stage, the caterpillar has two orange horns on its head. These horns give off a very bad smell. This scares away the caterpillar's enemies.

The Birdwing Butterfly

Birdwing butterflies live in the rain forests of Asia and Australia. The males are dark with lines of gold and green. The females are brown. The birdwing is the giant of the butterfly family. Its wingspan is about 11 inches.

Birdwings have very long front wings. Their rear wings are much shorter. When they fly, birdwings look like birds in the sky.

The Apollo Butterfly

The Apollo butterfly lives in the mountains of Europe. It is tan with orange and black dots on its wings. Its wingspan is about three inches. This butterfly took its name from Apollo, the Greek god of the sun. Like the Greek god, the Apollo butterfly likes the sun. It will fly only in bright sunshine. It hides when there are clouds in the sky.

Soon there may be few Apollo butterflies left in the world. They are in danger for several reasons. Air pollution kills many of the butterflies. The Apollo is also a "treasure" for many butterfly collectors. Many countries try to protect the Apollo butterflies. In some places it is now against the law to catch them.

Prefixes/Suffixes (1)

1. What does the word impossible mean in this passage?

   ◯ Wonderful
   ◯ Likely to happen
   ◯ Not possible
   ◯ Not pretty

Specialized/Technical Terms (1)

2. In this passage, the word wingspan means—

   ◯ a bird's size
   ◯ the distance between the tips of a bird's wings
   ◯ small, brown female butterfly
   ◯ a butterfly's front wings

Specialized/Technical Terms (1)

3. What does the word honeydew mean in this passage?

   ◯ The friendship between ants and common blue butterfly
   ◯ Sweet treat made by bees
   ◯ Food for common blue butterflies
   ◯ Sweet liquid made by caterpillar of the common blue butterfly

Facts/Details (2)

4. Which of the following butterflies will fly only in the sun?

   ◯ Common blue
   ◯ Swallowtail
   ◯ Birdwing
   ◯ Apollo

Facts/Details (2)

5. Where does the birdwing butterfly live?

   ⬭ Europe and Asia
   ⬭ Asia and Australia
   ⬭ Europe and Australia
   ⬭ Greece

Stated/Paraphrased Main Idea (3)

6. This passage is mostly about—

   ⬭ how caterpillars become butterflies
   ⬭ why ants protect common blue butterflies
   ⬭ some butterflies that live outside the United States
   ⬭ how butterflies get their names

Cause/Effect (4)

7. The Apollo butterfly may disappear from the earth because—

   ⬭ it likes to hide from the sun
   ⬭ it can only survive in bright sunshine
   ⬭ pollution and butterfly collectors put it in danger
   ⬭ its size is too small

Fact/Nonfact (6)

8. Which is a FACT in this passage?

   ⬭ There are about 20,000 kinds of butterflies.
   ⬭ There are more butterflies in Europe than Asia.
   ⬭ It would be wonderful to see all 20,000 kinds of butterflies.
   ⬭ Butterflies are beautiful insects.

Fact/Nonfact (6)

9. Which is an OPINION in this passage?

   ⬭ The swallowtail butterfly's wingspan is about four inches.
   ⬭ How wonderful it would be to see all 20,000 kinds of butterflies!
   ⬭ The birdwing butterfly is the largest butterfly in the world.
   ⬭ The Apollo butterfly lives in the mountains of Europe.

Title: The Boy Who Cried "Wolf"

Number of Words: 493

Objectives/Instructional Targets:

Objective 1:

- ☑ Use knowledge of the meanings of prefixes and suffixes to determine word meanings
- ☑ Use context clues to determine the meanings of unfamiliar words
- ☑ Use context clues to determine the meanings of specialized/technical terms

Objective 2:

- ❑ Recall supporting facts and details
- ☑ Arrange events in sequential order
- ❑ Follow written directions
- ☑ Describe the setting of a story (time and place)

Objective 3:

- ❑ Identify the stated or paraphrased main idea of a selection
- ☑ Identify the best summary of a selection

Objective 4:

- ❑ Identify cause and effect relationships
- ☑ Predict probable future outcomes

Objective 5:

- ☑ Understand the feelings and emotions of characters

Objective 6:

- ❑ Distinguish between fact and nonfact

The Boy Who Cried "Wolf"

Once there was a boy who cared for his village's sheep. Each morning he walked the sheep to one of the village fields. While the animals ate, the boy rested under a tree and watched over them. The greatest <u>threat</u> was from the wolf that lived in nearby hills. The boy had never seen the wolf, but he was always <u>alert</u> in case the wolf came too close.

The boy's job was important, but he hated it. There was really nothing wrong with the job. It was not hard or dirty work. He hated his job for one reason—it was boring. He spent many hours alone. There was no one to talk to or play with. Most of the time, the boy thought about his friends. Their jobs let them be near other people.

One day the boy decided to add some excitement to his life. He left the <u>flock</u> alone in the field and ran to the village. As he ran, he yelled, "Wolf! Wolf! The wolf is attacking!"

The <u>villagers</u> stopped their work and ran toward the field. They carried shovels, sticks, and rocks to fight the wolf. Of course, when they reached the field, there was no wolf. The boy sat in the grass and laughed. He had fooled them all!

"Why did you do this?" asked one man. "You frightened us! Don't do this again!"

The boy still thought it was a funny trick. He laughed and giggled as the people complained and walked back to the village.

For a while the boy was <u>content</u>. He sat under the tree, watched the sheep, and laughed about his trick. Before long, however, he became bored again. So, once again, he ran toward the village and yelled, "Wolf! Wolf! The wolf is attacking!"

Just as before, the people in the village ran to save the sheep. Of course, when they reached the field, again there was no wolf. And again, the boy laughed at the people.

"Why did you do this?" asked one man. "Someday you'll need our help, but no one will come. We'll know that it is only a trick."

This time the boy was truly sorry. He promised he would never trick the people again.

A few days later the boy was resting beneath a tree and watching the sheep. He heard a noise in the shrubs and turned to see what it was. At that moment, a wolf dashed from beneath the bushes and charged at the sheep. The boy wasted no time. He ran toward the village and yelled, "Wolf! Wolf! The wolf is attacking!"

The people in the village had been fooled twice. They were not about to be fooled again. They kept on with their work. Again and again the boy yelled, "Wolf! Wolf!"

The <u>villagers</u> did not answer his cries for help. The boy ran back to the field, but it was too late. The wolf had eaten the whole <u>flock</u> of sheep.

Unfamiliar Words (1)

1. In this passage, the word <u>threat</u> means—

- ⬯ kindness
- ⬯ work
- ⬯ danger
- ⬯ field

Unfamiliar Words (1)

2. What does the word <u>alert</u> mean in this passage?

- ⬯ Paying attention
- ⬯ Resting
- ⬯ Hiding
- ⬯ Asleep

Specialized/Technical Terms (1)

3. In this passage, the word <u>flock</u> means—

- ⬯ village
- ⬯ job
- ⬯ friends
- ⬯ group

Prefixes/Suffixes (1)

4. In this passage, the word <u>villagers</u> means people who—

- ⬯ watch sheep
- ⬯ work in the fields
- ⬯ live in a village
- ⬯ do not work

Unfamiliar Words (1)

5. In this passage, the word <u>content</u> means—

- ⬯ angry
- ⬯ happy
- ⬯ bored
- ⬯ scared

Sequential Order (2)

6. Which of the following happened first in this story?

- ⬯ The boy laughed at the people who came to help him.
- ⬯ The boy decided to add some excitement to his life.
- ⬯ The man told the boy not to frighten the people again.
- ⬯ The wolf ran from beneath the bushes.

Setting of Story (2)

7. Most of this story happened—

- ⬭ in the hills near a village
- ⬭ at the boy's home
- ⬭ in a house in a village
- ⬭ in a field near a village

Best Summary (3)

8. Which is the best summary of this story?

- ⬭ A boy cares for his village's sheep and scares away a wolf.
- ⬭ A wolf attacks a flock of sheep and scares a boy.
- ⬭ A boy pretends to be in trouble and then cannot get help when he needs it.
- ⬭ Several villagers try to save their sheep from a wolf.

Predicting Outcomes (4)

9. Which of the following will the boy probably do next?

- ⬭ Chase the wolf to the village
- ⬭ Return to the village and tell people the sheep are gone
- ⬭ Think of a new trick to play on people in the village
- ⬭ Look for new sheep to watch

Feelings/Emotions of Characters (5)

10. When the boy tricked the people in the village, he probably believed that the trick was—

- ⬭ harmless
- ⬭ dangerous
- ⬭ important
- ⬭ evil

Feelings/Emotions of Characters (5)

11. Why did the people ignore the boy's cries for help?

- ⬭ They wanted to scare the boy.
- ⬭ They did not care about the sheep.
- ⬭ They were afraid of the wolf.
- ⬭ They did not believe the wolf was nearby.

Reading
Answer Key

Page 13

"Oh, I am so sorry, sir, but you got in my way. If you had moved aside, I could have caught it," answered the man.

Birbal looked around, but saw nothing. "What were you trying to catch?" he asked the man.

"I had just said my evening prayers from that church over there. I was running to see how far my voice could reach. You ruined my chance, because you were in my way," the man explained.

"This is just too easy," Birbal laughed to himself. "Imagine a man chasing his own voice down the street!" He added the man's name and address to his paper and continued down the street.

Unfamiliar Words (1)

1. In this passage, the word <u>dashed</u> means—

   ○ walked slowly
   ○ stood still
   ○ jumped high
   ➡ ● ran quickly

Prefixes/Suffixes (1)

2. What does the word <u>pavement</u> mean in this story?

   ○ Church steps
   ➡ ● Street
   ○ Mud
   ○ Floor

Facts/Details (2)

3. The first foolish man that Birbal met was—

   ○ working in the king's court
   ○ riding a horse
   ➡ ● standing in a mud puddle
   ○ buying a pot at the market

Sequential Order (2)

4. Which event happened first in the story?

   ○ Birbal met a man riding a horse.
   ➡ ● Akbar said he wanted to see some foolish people.
   ○ Birbal wrote the man's name on a paper.
   ○ Birbal pulled the man from a mud puddle.

13

Page 14

Setting of Story (2)

5. Where did most of this part of the story happen?

   ➡ ● On the streets of an Indian city
   ○ On a farm
   ○ At Akbar's castle
   ○ At Birbal's house

Best Summary (3)

6. Which is the best summary of this part of the story?

   ○ Akbar becomes a strong and fair king in India.
   ○ A man stands in a mud puddle and cannot get out.
   ○ Birbal meets a foolish man who carries a bale of hay on his head.
   ➡ ● Akbar's servant, Birbal, sets out to find six foolish people for the king.

Cause/Effect (4)

7. The man on the narrow street knocked Birbal down because he—

   ○ wanted to prove he was not foolish
   ○ did not like Birbal
   ➡ ● was trying to catch his voice
   ○ was late getting to his church

Predicting Outcomes (4)

8. Which of the following is Birbal most likely to do next?

   ○ Tell Akbar he could not find any foolish people
   ➡ ● Continue looking for more foolish people
   ○ Tell the three men that they are foolish
   ○ Chase the foolish man who knocked him down

Feelings/Emotions of Characters (5)

9. Birbal seems to think that finding six foolish people will be—

   ○ difficult
   ○ dangerous
   ○ scary
   ➡ ● easy

Feelings/Emotions of Characters (5)

10. How did the man feel after he knocked Birbal down?

   ➡ ● Sorry
   ○ Embarrassed
   ○ Disappointed
   ○ Foolish

14

Page 17

too, began to laugh. Birbal had pulled off a very funny <u>prank</u>!

The four other foolish people received gifts from Akbar, and Birbal was the star of the king's court for many days.

Prefixes/Suffixes (1)

1. In this passage, the word <u>approached</u> means—

   ○ went away
   ○ stood still
   ➡ ● went near
   ○ hid from

Unfamiliar Words (1)

2. What does the word <u>fortune</u> mean in this passage?

   ○ Behavior
   ○ Writing
   ➡ ● Luck
   ○ Thinking

Prefixes/Suffixes (1)

3. In this passage, what does the word <u>fulfilled</u> mean?

   ➡ ● Kept
   ○ Forgotten
   ○ Found
   ○ Spoken

Unfamiliar Words (1)

4. In this passage, the word <u>conceiving</u> means—

   ○ remembering
   ○ looking for
   ○ missing
   ➡ ● thinking of

Unfamiliar Words (1)

5. In this passage, the word <u>prank</u> means—

   ○ answer
   ➡ ● trick
   ○ laugh
   ○ list

Sequential Order (2)

6. Which of the following happened right after Birbal introduced the four foolish men?

   ○ Akbar began to laugh at the foolish men.
   ○ Birbal became the star of the king's court.
   ➡ ● Akbar looked around for the two missing foolish people.
   ○ Birbal sent the messenger to find the last two foolish men.

17

Page 18

Setting of Story (2)

7. When did Akbar meet the foolish men that Birbal found?

   ○ Late at night
   ○ Many days after Birbal found them
   ○ The same day Birbal found them
   ➡ ● The day after Birbal found them

Cause/Effect (4)

8. The members of Akbar's court laughed because they—

   ○ knew Akbar was angry at Birbal
   ➡ ● thought Birbal's prank was funny
   ○ had never met foolish people
   ○ wanted to fill the room with laughter

Feelings/Emotions of Characters (5)

9. Other members of Akbar's court probably thought that Birbal's prank was—

   ➡ ● clever
   ○ foolish
   ○ stupid
   ○ dangerous

Feelings/Emotions of Characters (5)

10. How did Birbal feel after he found the fourth foolish person?

   ○ Foolish
   ○ Frightened
   ➡ ● Lucky
   ○ Proud

18

Page 21

Specialized/Technical Terms (1)

1. In this passage, the word <u>conifers</u> means trees that—

   - grow in forests
   - lose their leaves
   - have seeds
   → ● make cones

Specialized/Technical Terms (1)

2. In this passage, the word <u>deciduous</u> describes trees that—

   - have needles
   → ● lose their leaves in winter
   - grow in rain forests
   - give us oxygen

Unfamiliar Words (1)

3. What does the word <u>towers</u> mean in this passage?

   → ● Stands tall
   - Cools
   - Gives
   - Stays green

Prefixes/Suffixes (1)

4. What does the word <u>coating</u> mean in this passage?

   - leaf
   → ● layer
   - cone
   - needle

Facts/Details (2)

5. Which of the following trees grows in a rain forest?

   - Spruce tree
   - Oak tree
   → ● Rubber tree
   - Poplar tree

Facts/Details (2)

6. The leaves on conifers are called—

   - cones
   - seeds
   → ● needles
   - firs

21

Page 22

Stated/Paraphrased Main Idea (3)

7. This passage is mostly about—

   - why people need oxygen
   - why forests are dark and scary
   - how trees live through the winter
   → ● the different kinds of forests in the world

Cause/Effect (4)

8. The needles on an evergreen tree are protected from the cold because the needles—

   - grow near the cones
   - drop seeds on the ground
   - are always green
   → ● have a waxy coating

Predicting Outcomes (4)

9. What would probably happen if there were no trees?

   - There would be no oxygen on the earth.
   → ● People would have to find new material to make some of the things they use.
   - There would be no green plants left on the earth.
   - The earth would become very cold.

Fact/Nonfact (6)

10. Which is an OPINION in the passage?

   → ● Rain forests are the most important forests on the earth.
   - Forests cover about one-fourth of the earth's land.
   - Oxygen is a gas that people need to breathe.
   - A rain forest may have thousands of different trees.

22

Page 25

Prefixes/Suffixes (1)

1. What does the word <u>inventor</u> mean in this passage?

   - A person who is famous
   → ● A person who creates new machines
   - A person who paints
   - A person who travels

Unfamiliar Words (1)

2. In this passage, the word <u>gadgets</u> means—

   - paintings
   - drawings
   → ● machines
   - ideas

Prefixes/Suffixes (1)

3. In this passage, the word <u>foresaw</u> means—

   - saw later
   → ● saw beforehand
   - did not see
   - looked back to

Unfamiliar Words (1)

4. What does the word <u>cast</u> mean in this passage?

   - Hid
   - Drew
   - Burned
   → ● Created

Facts/Details (2)

5. In addition to being an inventor, Leonardo da Vinci was also a—

   - farmer
   - soldier
   → ● painter
   - diver

Stated/Paraphrased Main Idea (3)

6. This passage is mostly about—

   - how da Vinci became a great artist
   - why da Vinci's inventions did not succeed
   - how da Vinci's inventions have changed in 500 years
   → ● some of da Vinci's creative inventions

25

Page 26

Cause/Effect (4)

7. According to the passage, da Vinci invented things because he—

   - did not enjoy painting
   → ● wanted easier and better ways to do things
   - knew no one else had good ideas
   - could never make most of his ideas

Fact/Nonfact (6)

8. Which is an OPINION in this passage?

   → ● Leonardo da Vinci had many, many wonderful ideas.
   - Leonardo da Vinci was a painter and an inventor.
   - Leonardo da Vinci lived more than 500 years ago.
   - Leonardo da Vinci made each of his inventions.

Fact/Nonfact (6)

9. Which is a FACT in this passage?

   - Leonardo da Vinci was one of the greatest painters in history.
   - Leonardo da Vinci knew the easiest and best way to work.
   → ● Leonardo da Vinci was born in Florence, Italy.
   - Leonardo da Vinci's most wonderful invention was the movie projector.

26

The first big chess <u>tournament</u> was in London, England. Adolf Anderssen, a German man, won this first contest. After a major <u>tournament</u> in Russia, the winner earned the title of "grandmaster." Today, anyone who wins a chess <u>tournament</u> is still called a grandmaster.

Paul Morphy was the first American chess champion. He was a great player. Morphy beat most of the great players from Europe. In fact, he never lost a game. Bobby Fischer was another famous chess champion. He learned to play chess when he was six years old. He was only 13 years old when he became the junior chess champion of the United States. He was the youngest grandmaster of all time.

Unfamiliar Words (1)

1. In this passage, the word <u>defeat</u> means—

   ○ like
   ○ help
   → ● beat
   ○ win

Specialized/Technical Terms (1)

2. What does the word <u>rook</u> mean in this passage?

   ○ King
   → ● Castle
   ○ Pawn
   ○ Piece

Unfamiliar Words (1)

3. In this passage, the word <u>strategies</u> means—

   ○ chess books
   ○ chess sets
   ○ players
   → ● careful plans

Specialized/Technical Terms (1)

4. In this passage, the word <u>tournaments</u> means—

   ○ best players
   → ● chess contests
   ○ kings and princes
   ○ people who play chess

Facts/Details (2)

5. What is it called when a player captures another player's king?

   ○ Grandmaster
   ○ Strategies
   ○ Capture
   → ● Checkmate

Facts/Details (2)

6. Where did the game of chess begin?

   ○ England
   ○ Germany
   → ● India
   ○ United States

Stated/Paraphrased Main Idea (3)

7. The second paragraph is mostly about—

   ○ how to win a chess game
   ○ how to capture a player's queen
   → ● why chess is like a war
   ○ why two people must play chess

Cause/Effect (4)

8. The game of chess spread around the world because—

   ○ Bobby Fischer taught people how to play
   → ● travelers took the game back to their homes
   ○ it began in the Indus Valley
   ○ it changed as time passed

Fact/Nonfact (6)

9. Which is a FACT in this passage?

   ○ The rules for chess are easy.
   ○ Chess is played like checkers.
   ○ Only royalty can play chess.
   → ● Paul Morphy was the first American chess champion.

Fact/Nonfact (6)

10. Which is an OPINION in this passage?

    ○ Chess is a game for two players.
    → ● Paul Morphy was a great player.
    ○ Bobby Fischer was the youngest grandmaster.
    ○ There are six different kinds of chess pieces.

Sojourner traveled and taught about kindness and truth. She met important people like William Lloyd Garrison. He was an <u>abolitionist</u>. This was a person who wanted to get rid of slavery. She also met a black man named Frederick Douglass, another <u>abolitionist</u>. Sojourner talked to them about slavery. Soon she also began to speak out against slavery. She became one of the most popular speakers in the country.

The End of a Great Life

Sojourner worked for many years. She taught former slaves and worked at a hospital for former slaves. In 1878, she stopped traveling. She was very old. Her health was not good.

Sojourner Truth died on November 26, 1883. She was a remarkable woman. She had done many great things for the country. Today, people still learn about her work. Truly, she was a "traveler for truth."

Unfamiliar Words (1)

1. In this passage, the word <u>master</u> means—

   ○ helper
   ○ slave
   → ● owner
   ○ parent

Prefixes/Suffixes

2. What does the word <u>abolitionist</u> mean in this passage?

   ○ A person who owned slaves
   ○ A person who sold slaves
   → ● A person who wanted to get rid of slavery
   ○ A person who had been a slave

Prefixes/Suffixes (1)

3. In this passage, the word <u>stunned</u> means—

   → ● surprised
   ○ free
   ○ sad
   ○ protected

Facts/Details (2)

4. When did Isabella move to New York City?

   ○ 1797
   ○ 1808
   ○ 1824
   → ● 1829

Sequential Order (2)

5. Isabella changed her name—

   ○ before moving to New York City
   → ● after leaving New York City
   ○ right after she became free
   ○ after she met William Lloyd Garrison

Best Summary (3)

6. Which is the best summary of this passage?

   ○ Isabella's parents fought hard to protect the only child they could keep.
   ○ Slave masters were cruel people and did not want to free their slaves.
   ○ Isabella moved to New York and taught young people.
   → ● Sojourner Truth was once a slave, but she gained her freedom and helped many people.

Cause/Effect (4)

7. Isabella left New York City because—

   ○ she had finished all the work she could do
   ○ she wanted to work with William Lloyd Garrison
   → ● she thought the city was a bad place for her son
   ○ she could not find a job there

Feelings/Emotions of Characters (5)

8. From information in the passage, Sojourner Truth seemed to be—

   ○ scared
   → ● helpful
   ○ mean
   ○ angry

Fact/Nonfact (6)

9. Which is an OPINION in this passage?

   → ● Sojourner Truth was a remarkable woman.
   ○ Sojourner Truth was once a slave.
   ○ Isabella had more than one master.
   ○ Sojourner Truth taught former slaves.

Fact/Nonfact (6)

10. Which is a FACT in this passage?

    ○ Sojourner Truth was always kind and honest.
    ○ Sojourner Truth was the most popular speaker in the country.
    → ● Sojourner Truth made speeches against slavery.
    ○ Sojourner Truth was very happy in New York City.

Page 37

Unfamiliar Words (1)

1. In this passage, the word <u>convenient</u> means—

   ○ hard
   ○ silly
   ○ long
   → ● easy

Unfamiliar Words (1)

2. What does the word <u>crisp</u> mean in this passage?

   → ● Hard
   ○ Soft
   ○ Thick
   ○ Sliced

Prefixes/Suffixes (1)

3. In this passage, the word <u>blunder</u> means—

   ○ waiter
   ○ surprise
   → ● mistake
   ○ hotel

Facts/Details (2)

4. The first sandwich was eaten at a—

   ○ hotel
   ○ concert
   → ● card game
   ○ grocery store

Sequential Order (2)

5. The chef served thin, dark toast to other guests—

   → ● after Nellie said it tasted wonderful
   ○ before he apologized to Nellie
   ○ just before Nellie ate her toast
   ○ before Nellie ordered toast

Best Summary (3)

6. Which is the best summary of this passage?

   ○ Foods get their names in many funny ways.
   ○ Sandwiches are very easy to eat.
   ○ Melba toast was caused by a chef's accident.
   → ● Some foods, like sandwiches and Melba toast, have been named for people.

Page 38

Cause/Effect (4)

7. John Montague asked for meat between two slices of bread because—

   ○ his servant did not know how to make other food
   → ● he wanted something he could eat at the card table
   ○ his servant had to make his lunch quickly
   ○ this was his favorite lunch

Feelings/Emotions of Characters (5)

8. When the waiter served burned toast to Nellie, how did the chef feel?

   ○ Angry
   ○ Proud
   ● Ashamed
   ○ Surprised

Fact/Nonfact (6)

9. Which is an OPINION in this passage?

   → ● It's fun to find out how foods got their names.
   ○ John Montague was the Fourth Earl of Sandwich.
   ○ The chef burned Nellie's toast on purpose.
   ○ John Montague liked sandwiches better than any other food.

Fact/Nonfact (6)

10. Which is a FACT in this passage?

    ○ John Montague played cards better than anyone else.
    ○ Melba toast is ordered more often than other kinds of toast.
    → ● Sandwich was an area in England.
    ○ Melba toast tastes wonderful.

Page 41

After working and working, the knights finally found one of the treasures. The Lord of the Sea feared they might find more. He wanted to stop them. He angrily turned all the knights into small crabs. But the knights had always been <u>loyal</u> to their king and his kingdom. They kept digging and digging in the sand.

"And that, Tommy, is why the little crabs still dig in the sand today," Grandfather said.

Tommy smiled and looked down at the sand...and the little crabs were still digging.

Unfamiliar Words (1)

1. In this passage, the word <u>dreary</u> means—

   ○ bright and cheery
   ○ sunny and warm
   ○ hot and windy
   → ● damp and cloudy

Unfamiliar Words (1)

2. What does the word <u>detail</u> mean in this passage?

   → ● Piece of information
   ○ Story
   ○ Adventure
   ○ Real story

Prefixes/Suffixes

3. In this passage, the word <u>conquered</u> means—

   ○ returned
   ○ lost
   → ● defeated
   ○ hid

Unfamiliar Words (1)

4. In this passage, the word <u>loyal</u> means—

   ○ greedy
   ○ angry
   → ● faithful
   ○ happy

Sequential Order (2)

5. What happened right after the king died?

   ○ The knights decided to give away his treasures.
   → ● The knights went to search for the buried treasures.
   ○ The knights buried the treasures in another place.
   ○ The knights fought a battle against the Lord of the Sea.

Page 42

Setting of Story (2)

6. Where is Grandfather when he tells Tommy this story?

   ○ In Tommy's house
   ○ At the king's castle
   ○ At his house
   → ● On the beach

Best Summary (3)

7. Which is the best summary of this story?

   ○ A grandfather and grandson walk on a beach and find tiny crabs.
   ○ A boy asks his grandfather to explain why crabs dig in the sand.
   → ● A grandfather's story gives a make-believe explanation of why crabs dig in the sand.
   ○ A king orders his knights to bury his treasure in the sand.

Cause/Effect (4)

8. The king hid all his treasures because he—

   ○ wanted his knights to look for the treasures
   → ● did not want people in his kingdom to become greedy
   ○ knew the Lord of the Sea wanted to steal them
   ○ did not want Tommy and his grandfather to find them

Feelings/Emotions of Characters (5)

9. How did Tommy feel about hearing his grandfather's story?

   ○ Uninterested
   ○ Bored
   ○ Nervous
   → ● Eager

Feelings/Emotions of Characters (5)

10. How did Grandfather probably feel about telling his story?

    → ● Pleased
    ○ Angry
    ○ Nervous
    ○ Useless

Page 45

can also ask someone else to ask you questions. Your mom, dad, or older brother or sister can ask questions about your work. This is a good time to summarize the work. Can you explain the main idea in a few words?

5. Finally, look over your work one last time. What was it about? Did you finish the whole assignment? Did you answer all your questions? What did you learn?

Why Use SQ3R

SQ3R can help you with any assignment. It will also help you be a more independent reader and learner. You will feel good about working on your own. You will be learning how to direct your own school work. And, you will probably become a better student. SQ3R is a study method you can use throughout your life.

Unfamiliar Words (1)

1. In this passage, the word <u>survey</u> means—

   ○ finish
   ○ write
   → ● look over
   ○ remember

Unfamiliar Words (1)

2. What does the word <u>recite</u> mean in this passage?

   → ● Give the answers
   ○ Stop studying
   ○ Write or read
   ○ Help someone

Prefixes/Suffixes (1)

3. In this passage, the word <u>summarize</u> means—

   ○ use many details
   ○ ask for help
   → ● present main ideas in a few words
   ○ take a rest

Prefixes/Suffixes (1)

4. In this passage, the word <u>independent</u> means—

   ○ needing help from others
   → ● able to work alone
   ○ slow and careful
   ○ interesting

45

Page 46

Sequential Order (2)

5. Which is the last step of SQ3R?

   ○ Explain each answer to your parents
   ○ Look at how the lesson is organized
   ○ Write your questions on paper
   → ● Look over your work one last time

Following Directions (2)

6. You should look over the questions before you begin an assignment because—

   ○ this is the only way to answer them
   → ● they can show you what the lesson is about
   ○ this will make you more independent
   ○ this is the fastest way to work

Stated/Paraphrased Main Idea (3)

7. This passage is mostly about—

   ○ the best way to get better grades
   ○ answering questions correctly
   → ● how to use SQ3R to study
   ○ how to improve your grades

Cause/Effect (4)

8. According to the passage, if you make up your own questions, then you will—

   → ● learn more
   ○ waste too much time
   ○ make your teacher happy
   ○ know what the assignment is

Predicting Outcomes (4)

9. What will probably happen if you learn and use SQ3R?

   ○ You will earn all A's on your report card.
   ○ Your teacher will give you more work.
   → ● You will become a better student.
   ○ You will spend less time on school work.

Fact/Nonfact (6)

10. Which is an OPINION in this passage?

    ○ The first step in SQ3R is to survey.
    → ● SQ3R is an easy way to study.
    ○ Everyone should study in the same way.
    ○ SQ3R has five steps.

46

Page 49

A Ladybug's Diet

A ladybug is no "lady" when it comes to eating. Every ladybug has a huge appetite. One adult ladybug may eat more than 50 insects in one day! Ladybugs eat many kinds of insects, including spider mites and scale ladybugs. Its favorite meal is the <u>aphid</u>.

The ladybug's diet makes it a friend to farmers and gardeners. It eats many of the insects that destroy crops. For example, <u>aphids</u>, or plant lice, live on plants and suck food from them. This can kill the plants. To protect their plants, many growers let ladybugs loose in their fields or gardens. The ladybugs eat the unwanted guests. In some places, people even have "ladybug farms." They raise ladybugs and sell them to growers who need them.

Ladybugs are colorful and helpful members of the insect world. If one lands on your shoulder, look at it carefully. You might also say, "Thanks for your help, little fatty."

Unfamiliar Words (1)

1. In this passage, the word <u>varieties</u> means—

   ○ insects
   ○ ladybugs
   ○ spots
   → ● different kinds

Specialized/Technical Terms (1)

2. What does the word <u>elytra</u> mean in this passage?

   ○ A ladybug's true wings
   ○ The spots on a ladybug's back
   → ● Outer coverings that protect a ladybug's wings
   ○ A ladybug's enemy

Prefixes/Suffixes (1)

3. In this passage, the word <u>defense</u> means—

   ○ color
   ○ surroundings
   → ● protection
   ○ markings

Specialized/Technical Terms (1)

4. In this passage, the word <u>aphids</u> means—

   → ● plant lice
   ○ farmers and gardeners
   ○ ladybug farms
   ○ unwanted insects

49

Page 50

Facts/Details (2)

5. How many kinds of ladybugs are in the world?

   ○ 20
   ○ 50
   ○ 100
   → ● 3,000

Facts/Details (2)

6. Reflex bleeding is how a ladybug—

   ○ blends in with its surroundings
   ○ makes colorful markings
   → ● makes a smell to keep its enemies away
   ○ lifts its wings

Sequential Order (2)

7. In order to fly, a ladybug must first—

   ○ release liquid from its legs
   → ● lift its hard shell
   ○ have at least seven spots
   ○ protect itself from enemies

Best Summary (3)

8. Which is the best summary of the sixth paragraph?

   ○ Ladybugs can blend in with their surroundings.
   → ● Ladybugs have several ways to protect themselves from their enemies.
   ○ Ladybugs are interesting and useful insects.
   ○ Ants and birds do not like the taste of ladybugs.

Cause/Effect (4)

9. Some farmers release ladybugs in their fields in order to—

   ○ give ladybugs a good diet
   ○ raise ladybugs and sell them to other farmers
   ○ make the surroundings more beautiful and interesting
   → ● get rid of insects that destroy crops

Fact/Nonfact (6)

10. Which is a FACT in this passage?

    ○ In China, people call ladybugs "little fatties."
    → ● Ladybugs can come in many different colors.
    ○ Ladybugs are the most important insects in the world.
    ○ Everyone in the world likes to look at ladybugs.

50

Page 53

Unfamiliar Words (1)

1. In this passage, the word <u>colonies</u> means—

   - ⚪ small mammals
   - → ⚫ groups of animals that live together
   - ⚪ pets that live in cages
   - ⚪ gerbils kept as pets

Specialized/Technical Terms (1)

2. What does the term <u>native habitats</u> mean in this passage?

   - ⚪ Gerbil cages
   - ⚪ Deserts in Asia
   - → ⚫ Natural living areas
   - ⚪ Homes for pets

Prefixes/Suffixes (1)

3. In this passage, the word <u>bedding</u> means—

   - ⚪ a 10-gallon aquarium
   - ⚪ old newspaper
   - → ⚫ material used to make a bed
   - ⚪ a place to sleep

Prefixes/Suffixes (1)

4. What does the word <u>vegetarian</u> mean in this passage?

   - ⚪ Containing only meat
   - → ⚫ Containing only vegetables
   - ⚪ A special treat
   - ⚪ Containing pet food

Facts/Details (2)

5. Which of the following is a good choice for a gerbil's bedding?

   - ⚪ Dandelions
   - ⚪ Newspaper
   - ⚪ Sand
   - → ⚫ Wood Chips

Following Directions (2)

6. Since gerbils like to chew on things, you should—

   - ⚪ give them only soft foods
   - ⚪ use plastic toys they cannot destroy
   - ⚪ clean their houses every two weeks
   - → ⚫ give them wood to chew

53

Page 54

Stated/Paraphrased Main Idea (3)

7. The fifth paragraph is mostly about—

   - → ⚫ good toys for gerbils
   - ⚪ why gerbils need to exercise
   - ⚪ watching gerbils play
   - ⚪ why gerbils like to hide

Cause/Effect (4)

8. A gerbil's house should not be in direct sunlight because—

   - ⚪ gerbils cannot sleep in the sunlight
   - ⚪ gerbils chew more when in direct sunlight
   - → ⚫ too much heat can hurt gerbils
   - ⚪ the gerbil's food will spoil

Fact/Nonfact (6)

9. Which is an OPINION in this passage?

   - ⚪ Gerbils need plastic toys.
   - → ⚫ Gerbils are easy to care for.
   - ⚪ Gerbils are really desert animals.
   - ⚪ Gerbils need fresh water every day.

54

Page 57

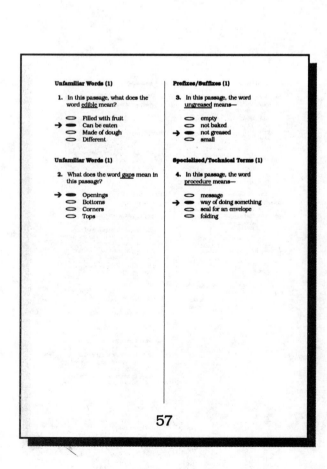

Unfamiliar Words (1)

1. In this passage, what does the word <u>edible</u> mean?

   - ⚪ Filled with fruit
   - → ⚫ Can be eaten
   - ⚪ Made of dough
   - ⚪ Different

Unfamiliar Words (1)

2. What does the word <u>gaps</u> mean in this passage?

   - → ⚫ Openings
   - ⚪ Bottoms
   - ⚪ Corners
   - ⚪ Tops

Prefixes/Suffixes (1)

3. In this passage, the word <u>ungreased</u> means—

   - ⚪ empty
   - ⚪ not baked
   - → ⚫ not greased
   - ⚪ small

Specialized/Technical Terms (1)

4. In this passage, the word <u>procedure</u> means—

   - ⚪ message
   - → ⚫ way of doing something
   - ⚪ seal for an envelope
   - ⚪ folding

57

Page 58

Sequential Order (2)

5. What should you do right after folding down the top corner of the dough envelope?

   - ⚪ Make a seal for the envelope
   - ⚪ Stuff the envelope with fruit
   - ⚪ Bake the envelope on a cookie sheet
   - → ⚫ Check for gaps that could leak

Following Directions (2)

6. When making these snacks, you should—

   - ⚪ only use a cheese or fruit filling
   - → ⚫ let them cool after baking
   - ⚪ make another set of snacks
   - ⚪ eat them as soon as possible

Stated/Paraphrased Main Idea (3)

7. This passage is mostly about—

   - ⚪ why you should eat vegetables and fruits
   - ⚪ choosing the right fillings for the snacks
   - → ⚫ making envelope-shaped snacks
   - ⚪ how to mail something in an envelope

Fact/Nonfact (6)

8. Which is an OPINION in this passage?

   - → ⚫ Fruit envelopes taste delicious when served with ice cream.
   - ⚪ Papers, bills, and letters can be kept in real envelopes.
   - ⚪ Pie dough is used to make this snack.
   - ⚪ You can mail this envelope snack to people.

58

Page 61

Plant bluebonnet seeds in the fall. Do not plant them very deep in the soil. Scatter the seed in a place that gets lots of sun in the spring. Use a rake to spread a thin layer of dirt over the seeds. In the spring, you should have your first crop of bluebonnets.

If you want more and more bluebonnets each year, it is best not to pick the flowers. Let the flowers die on the plants. The dying flowers will drop their seeds in the soil. Next year, you will have even more lovely bluebonnets to enjoy!

Unfamiliar Words (1)

1. What does the word <u>varieties</u> mean in this passage?

- Flowers
➡ ● Kinds
- Leaves
- States

Unfamiliar Words (1)

2. In this passage, the word <u>phrase</u> means—

- tiny flowers
- bluebonnet
➡ ● group of words
- wolf flower

Specialized/Technical Words (1)

3. In this passage, the word <u>scientific</u> means—

- like a flower
- not like science
- belonging to plants
➡ ● from science

Prefixes/Suffixes (1)

4. In this passage, what does the word <u>unlike</u> mean?

- Special
- Very old
➡ ● Not the same as
- Not in Texas

61

Page 62

Unfamiliar Words (1)

5. In this passage, the word <u>fragance</u> means—

➡ ● smell
- stem
- color
- soil

Facts/Details (2)

6. When should bluebonnet seeds be planted?

- Early spring
- March
- Late summer
➡ ● Fall

Following Directions (2)

7. Bluebonnet seeds should be planted—

- deep in the soil
- along the highway
➡ ● in sunny places
- away from other flowers

Stated/Paraphrased Main Idea (3)

8. The second paragraph is mostly about—

- the correct name for a bluebonnet
- why people call the bluebonnet "el conejo"
➡ ● different names given to the bluebonnet
- why the bluebonnet became the state flower

Cause/Effect (4)

9. Why should you let the flowers die on the bluebonnet plants?

- So prettier flowers will grow in the spring
➡ ● So the flowers will drop their seeds in the soil
- So the flowers will be real wildflowers
- So other flowers cannot grow

Fact/Nonfact (6)

10. Which is an OPINION in the passage?

➡ ● Bluebonnets have a nice smell.
- Bluebonnets were called buffalo clover.
- Bluebonnet flowers can be pink and white.
- The bluebonnet is the state flower of Texas.

62

Page 65

Specialized/Technical Terms (1)

1. In this passage, the word <u>conduct</u> means—

- remove
- save
- cover
➡ ● carry

Prefixes/Suffixes (1)

2. What does the word <u>motorists</u> mean?

- People who fly kites
- People who are in the street
➡ ● People who drive cars
- People who follow rules

Unfamiliar Words (1)

3. In this passage, the word <u>retrieve</u> means—

➡ ● go and get
- drop
- drive on a road
- fly a kite

Facts/Details (2)

4. Which of the following is the best kind of string for a kite?

- Wire
- Metal
➡ ● Cotton
- Plastic

Following Directions (2)

5. What should you do if your kite lands on power lines?

- Climb carefully and get the kite
- Move to an open area
- Ask a driver to help you
➡ ● Leave the kite and report the problem to the power company

Following Directions (3)

6. To be safe, you should fly your kite—

- near streets and roads
➡ ● in a large, open area
- close to local power lines
- on the school grounds

65

Page 66

Best Summary (3)

7. Which is the best summary of this passage?

- Kite-flying is a great way to spend a breezy day.
- Kites can be made of many different materials like wood, plastic, and paper.
➡ ● There are important safety rules to follow when you fly a kite.
- You should fly a kite away from power lines and roads.

Cause Effect (4)

8. You should not fly a kite in the rain or a storm because—

- your kite could get wet
➡ ● lightning could injure you
- you will be scared
- drivers will not see you

Fact/Nonfact (6)

9. Which of the following is an OPINION in this passage?

- You should fly a kite away from power lines.
- Kites can be made of plastic, wood, or paper.
- If a kite touches a power line, it could conduct electricity to your body.
➡ ● It's always fun to watch a colorful kite soar and dive in the sky.

Fact/Nonfact (6)

10. Which is a FACT in this passage?

➡ ● Kites should not have metal parts.
- Kite-flying is a great way to spend a breezy day.
- Kite-flying is enjoyable.
- Plastic is the best material for a kite.

66

Page 69

Specialized/Technical Terms (1)

1. In this passage, the word prehensile means—

   ○ attached to the body
   → ● used like a hand
   ○ shaped like a horse's head
   ○ long and thin

Specialized/Technical Terms (1)

2. What does the word dorsal mean in this passage?

   ○ In a pouch
   ○ Unlike other fish
   ○ Upright in the water
   → ● On the back

Unfamiliar Words (1)

3. In this passage, the word pouch means a—

   ○ group of baby seahorses
   → ● pocket on the front of the body
   ○ male seahorse
   ○ seahorse's eggs

Specialized/Technical Terms (1)

4. In this passage, the word plankton means—

   → ● tiny animals floating in the ocean
   ○ a seahorse's eye
   ○ seaweed and other plants
   ○ a way to search for food

Unfamiliar Words (1)

5. What does the word camouflage mean in this passage?

   ○ Looking for enemies
   ○ Searching for food
   → ● Hiding by changing colors
   ○ Bony and hard to eat

Facts/Details (2)

6. According to this passage, the largest seahorse—

   ○ lives in the Gulf of Mexico
   ○ is only one inch long
   → ● is more than one foot long
   ○ does not eat plankton

69

Page 70

Facts/Details (2)

7. A male seahorse carries the female's eggs in its—

   ○ head
   → ● pouch
   ○ tail
   ○ fin

Stated/Paraphrased Main Idea (3)

8. This passage is mostly about—

   ○ why seahorses have few enemies
   ○ how seahorses swim in the water
   ○ how baby seahorses are born
   → ● why seahorses are unusual fish

Cause/Effect (4)

9. A seahorse changes colors so it can—

   ○ look like other fish
   ○ carry eggs in its pouch
   → ● hide from other animals
   ○ eat more plankton

Fact/Nonfact (6)

10. Which is an OPINION in this passage?

   ○ There are more than 30 kinds of seahorses.
   ○ Some seahorses are only one inch long.
   ○ Seahorses hold on to things with their tails.
   → ● The seahorse is a very different kind of fish.

70

Page 73

The country mouse could feel his heart thumping against his chest. He looked at his cousin, who seemed to be shaking. He could not stand it.

"I am sorry, cousin," said the country mouse. "You were kind to invite me, but I cannot stay. I am so frightened. I would never be able to eat."

"Look at all that wonderful food," answered the city mouse. "The people will leave soon. Then we can have our feast."

"That may be true," the country mouse said, "but I am not willing to pay your price. I would rather eat my beans and roots in peace." With those words, the country mouse slipped out the door and ran home to the country.

Prefixes/Suffixes (1)

1. In this passage, the word displeased means—

   ○ very glad
   ○ not quick
   → ● not happy
   ○ very honest

Unfamiliar Words (1)

2. What does the word scurried mean in this passage?

   → ● Ran quickly
   ○ Hid
   ○ Started to eat
   ○ Listened carefully

Unfamiliar Words (1)

3. In this passage, the word slipped means—

   ○ stood
   ○ yelled loudly
   ○ entered
   → ● went quietly

73

Page 74

Sequential Order (2)

4. What happened right after the two mice sat to eat the first time?

   ○ They talked about the wonderful food.
   ○ They scurried behind the stove.
   → ● They heard human footsteps.
   ○ They saw someone in the doorway.

Setting of Story (2)

5. Where did this story happen?

   ○ In Greece long ago
   ○ In the city
   ○ In the country
   → ● In both the city and the country

Cause/Effect (4)

6. The country mouse went back to his home because—

   ○ he did not like the city mouse's food
   → ● he was too scared in the city
   ○ the city mouse asked him to leave
   ○ his food tasted better than the city mouse's food

Predicting Outcomes (4)

7. Which of the following will the city mouse and country mouse most likely do?

   ○ Decide to live together in the city
   ○ Visit each other every day
   → ● Stay in their own homes
   ○ Trade food with each other

Feelings/Emotions of Characters (5)

8. When the city mouse saw the country mouse's food, he felt—

   ○ excited
   ○ silly
   → ● disappointed
   ○ angry

Feelings/Emotions of Characters (5)

9. When the country mouse returned to his home, he probably felt—

   ○ frightened
   → ● happy
   ○ jealous
   ○ angry

74

The Apollo Butterfly

The Apollo butterfly lives in the mountains of Europe. It is tan with orange and black dots on its wings. Its wingspan is about three inches. This butterfly took its name from Apollo, the Greek god of the sun. Like the Greek god, the Apollo butterfly likes the sun. It will fly only in bright sunshine. It hides when there are clouds in the sky.

Soon there may be few Apollo butterflies left in the world. They are in danger for several reasons. Air pollution kills many of the butterflies. The Apollo is also a "treasure" for many butterfly collectors. Many countries try to protect the Apollo butterflies. In some places it is now against the law to catch them.

Prefixes/Suffixes (1)

1. What does the word impossible mean in this passage?

- Wonderful
- Likely to happen
- → Not possible
- Not pretty

Specialized/Technical Terms (1)

2. In this passage, the word wingspan means—

- a bird's size
- → the distance between the tips of a bird's wings
- small, brown female butterfly
- a butterfly's front wings

Specialized/Technical Terms (1)

3. What does the word honeydew mean in this passage?

- The freindship between ants and common blue butterfly
- Sweet treat made by bees
- Food for common blue butterflies
- → Sweet liquid made by caterpillar of the common blue butterfly

Facts/Details (2)

4. Which of the following butterflies will fly only in the sun?

- Common blue
- Swallowtail
- Birdwing
- → Apollo

77

Facts/Details (2)

5. Where does the birdwing butterfly live?

- Europe and Asia
- → Asia and Australia
- Europe and Australia
- Greece

Stated/Paraphrased Main Idea (3)

6. This passage is mostly about—

- how caterpillars become butterflies
- why ants protect common blue butterflies
- → some butterflies that live outside the United States
- how butterflies get their names

Cause/Effect (4)

7. The Apollo butterfly may disappear from the earth because—

- it likes to hide from the sun
- it can only survive in bright sunshine
- → pollution and butterfly collectors put it in danger
- its size is too small

Fact/Nonfact (6)

8. Which is a FACT in this passage?

- → There are about 20,000 kinds of butterflies.
- There are more butterflies in Europe than Asia.
- It would be wonderful to see all 20,000 kinds of butterflies.
- Butterflies are beautiful insects.

Fact/Nonfact (6)

9. Which is an OPINION in this passage?

- The swallowtail butterfly's wingspan is about four inches.
- → How wonderful it would be to see all 20,000 kinds of butterflies!
- The birdwing butterfly is the largest butterfly in the world.
- The Apollo butterfly lives in the mountains of Europe.

78

Unfamiliar Words (1)

1. In this passage, the word threat means—

- kindness
- work
- → danger
- field

Unfamiliar Words (1)

2. What does the word alert mean in this passage?

- → Paying attention
- Resting
- Hiding
- Asleep

Specialized/Technical Terms (1)

3. In this passage, the word flock means—

- village
- job
- friends
- → group

Prefixes/Suffixes (1)

4. In this passage, the word villagers means people who—

- watch sheep
- work in the fields
- → live in a village
- do not work

Unfamiliar Words (1)

5. In this passage, the word content means—

- angry
- → happy
- bored
- scared

Sequential Order (2)

6. Which of the following happened first in this story?

- The boy laughed at the people who came to help him.
- → The boy decided to add some excitement to his life.
- The man told the boy not to frighten the people again.
- The wolf ran from beneath the bushes.

81

Setting of Story (2)

7. Most of this story happened—

- in the hills near a village
- at the boy's home
- in a house in a village
- → in a field near a village

Best Summary (3)

8. Which is the best summary of this story?

- A boy cares for his village's sheep and scares away a wolf.
- A wolf attacks a flock of sheep and scares a boy.
- → A boy pretends to be in trouble and then cannot get help when he needs it.
- Several villagers try to save their sheep from a wolf.

Predicting Outcomes (4)

9. Which of the following will the boy probably do next?

- Chase the wolf to the village
- → Return to the village and tell people the sheep are gone
- Think of a new trick to play on people in the village
- Look for new sheep to watch

Feelings/Emotions of Characters (5)

10. When the boy tricked the people in the village, he probably believed that the trick was—

- → harmless
- dangerous
- important
- evil

Feelings/Emotions of Characters (5)

11. Why did the people ignore the boy's cries for help?

- They wanted to scare the boy.
- They did not care about the sheep.
- They were afraid of the wolf.
- → They did not believe the wolf was nearby.

82

More Quality Products from ECS

ECS Learning Systems, a Texas company based in San Antonio, is the leading publisher of TAAS practice materials. We also offer a complete line of creative educational resource books and magazines that teach important writing, reading, math, and thinking skills.

Other Resources from ECS

CATALOG NUMBER	TITLE/ DESCRIPTION	UNIT PRICE
	Writing	
ECS9617	Booklinks Gr. 3-8	$13.95
ECS9900	Foundations for Writing, Book 1 Gr. 2-5	$16.95
ECS0476	Foundations for Writing, Book 2 Gr. 3-8	$17.95
ECS9609	Inkblots Gr. 6-12	$13.95
ECS0484	Not More Writing?! Gr. 9-12	$17.95
ECS9625	Passageways Gr. 5-9	$12.95
ECS9072	Writing Warm-Ups™ Gr. K-6	$10.95
ECS9080	Writing Warm-Ups™ Gr. 7-12	$10.95
ECS9455	Writing Warm-Ups™ Two Gr. K-6	$10.95
ECS9463	Writing Warm-Ups™ Two Gr. 7-12	$10.95
	Writing Teacher™ magazine Gr. K-8	$25 (1 yr.)
	Reading	
ECS9722	Bluebonnet Books 1 ('93-'94) Gr. 3-8	$16.95
ECS0034	Bluebonnet Books 2 ('94-'95) Gr. 3-8	$17.95
ECS951X	Building Language Power I Gr. 4-9	$12.95
ECS9528	Building Language Power II Gr. 4-9	$12.95
ECS9684	Building Language Power III Gr. 4-9	$12.95
ECS000X	Novel Extenders, Book 1 Gr. 1-3	$15.95
ECS0018	Novel Extenders, Book 2 Gr. 1-3	$16.95
ECS0069	Novel Extenders, Book 3 Gr. 1-3	$15.95
ECS0077	Novel Extenders, Book 4 Gr. 1-3	$15.95
ECS0506	Novel Extenders: African-American Coll. Gr. 4-6	$14.95
ECS9587	Picture Book Companion I Gr. K-3	$12.95
ECS9595	Picture Book Companion II Gr. K-3	$12.95
ECS9641	Picture Book Companion III Gr. K-3	$12.95
ECS9692	Springboards for Reading Gr. 3-6	$11.95
ECS9706	Springboards for Reading Gr. 7-12	$10.95
	Thinking Skills	
ECS9676	Destinations Gr. 5-9	$13.95
ECS9633	Odysseys Gr. 5-9	$12.95
ECS9471	Quick Thinking™ Gr. K-6	$11.95
ECS948X	Quick Thinking™ Gr. 7-12	$11.95
ECS9439	Tactics to Tackle Thinking Gr. 7-12	$10.95
ECS9668	Voyages Gr. 5-9	$13.95
	THINK™ magazine All levels	$20 (1 yr.)

Also available: EnviroLearn™: 5 titles for Gr. K/1–5
Thematic Units: 16 titles for primary grades • 4 titles for intermediate and middle grades
Booklinks to American History Gr. 4-8: 8 titles • Booklinks to World History Gr. 4-8: 4 titles

New Home Study Collection™
for Grades 1-6   Only $4.95 ea.

Excellent Home Companions for TAAS Preparation!

This collection contains language arts, math, and reading activity books for the home. It's what parents have been searching for! Now parents can help their kids review, practice, extend, and enhance the skills they need to know in school.

Recommend these books to the parents!

Each title contains: Fun activities • Challenging and interesting lessons. • Learning activities for family involvement • Parent pull-out section with helpful hints, answer keys, and skill chart • Achievement award for the child

Look for ECS books at your local bookstore.
If they are not available, contact ECS Learning Systems, Inc. for a complete catalog.

ECS Learning Systems, Inc. • P.O. Box 791437 • San Antonio, TX 78279-1437 • 1-800-68-TEACH

NEW for TAAS

ECS Learning Systems Announces the NEW
TAAS Master™ Practice Tests
Great for practice and/or diagnosis

The TAAS Master™ Practice Tests are designed to assist teachers in diagnosing students' strengths and weaknesses on objectives for the Texas Assessment of Academic Skills (TAAS). Used as an informal diagnostic tool, the practice tests can help teachers identify the specific areas that students understand and those that may require further study or review before the actual test. Teachers can use the practice test results to plan and implement an effective instructional program for students. TAAS Master™ books many be used for remediation.

The TAAS Master™ Practice Tests include test items that address every objective for the given subject area (reading, mathematics, or writing). Each instructional target is represented by at least one item on the practice test. Since an instructional target may be tested in a variety of ways, the practice test items may not include every eligible type of item for a particular instructional target.

The TAAS Master™ Practice Tests are **not** designed to teach students "test-taking" skills (e.g.,"bubbling in" answers). Each practice test focuses on the **content** included in the TAAS test and provides information about students' understanding of the TAAS objectives.

Teachers may administer the TAAS Master™ Practice Test at any time during the school year.

Order Now only $29.95 ea.

Each **TAAS Master™ Practice Test Class Pack** includes: 30 consumable tests and a teacher's guide.

Catalog	Grade & Subject	Catalog	Grade & Subject
ECS0611	Grade 3 Math	ECS0654	Grade 7 Math
ECS0670	Grade 3 Reading	ECS0719	Grade 7 Reading
ECS0735	Grade 4 Writing	ECS0662	Grade 8 Math
ECS062X	Grade 4 Math	ECS0727	Grade 8 Reading
ECS0689	Grade 4 Reading	ECS0743	Grade 8 Writing
ECS0638	Grade 5 Math	ECS0751	Exit Math
ECS0697	Grade 5 Reading	ECS076X	Exit Reading
ECS0646	Grade 6 Math	ECS0778	Exit Writing
ECS0700	Grade 6 Reading		

Order Today!
All levels are available NOW!